CANADIAN GRAMMAR SPECTRUM

REFERENCE AND PRACTICE

John Eastwood

OXFORD
UNIVERSITY PRESS

OXFORD
UNIVERSITY PRESS

Oxford University Press is a department of the University of Oxford.
It furthers the University's objective of excellence in research, scholarship, and education by publishing worldwide.
Oxford is a registered trade mark of Oxford University Press in the UK and in certain other countries.

Published in Canada by
Oxford University Press
8 Sampson Mews, Suite 204,
Don Mills, Ontario M3C 0H5 Canada

www.oupcanada.com

Library and Archives Canada Cataloguing in Publication

Eastwood, John
Canadian grammar spectrum 4 : reference and practice / John Eastwood.

Includes index.
Previously published as part of: Eastwood, John. Oxford
practice grammar.
Intermediate, 2006.
ISBN 978-0-19-544833-7

1. English language—Grammar—Problems, exercises, etc.
2. English language—Textbooks for second language learners. I. Title.

PE1128.E26 2011   428.2'4   C2011-903940-0

Printed and bound in Canada.

1   2   3   4   —   15   14   13   12

Passive

Passive verb forms   50

Have something done   52

The Infinitive and the **-ing** form

Verb + **to**-infinitive   54

Verb + **-ing** form   56

Nouns and articles

Countable and uncountable nouns   58

A carton of milk, a piece of information, etc.   60

Nouns that can be countable or uncountable   62

Singular or plural?   64

A/an and **the**   66

Place names and **the**   68

This, my, some, a lot of, etc.

This, that, these, and **those**   72

My, your, etc. and **mine, yours,** etc.   74

Some and **any**   76

A lot of, lots of, many, much, (a) few, and **(a) little**   78

Pronouns

Personal pronouns   80

There and **it**   82

The pronoun **one/ones**   84

Adjectives and adverbs

Adjectives   86

Adjective order   88

Comparative and superlative forms   90

Adverbs of degree   94

Contents

	page
Introduction	1

Words and sentences

Word classes: nouns, verbs, adjectives, etc.	2
Sentence structure: subject, verb, object, etc.	4
Direct and indirect objects	6

Verbs

Simple Present	8
Present Progressive	10
Simple Past	12
Past Progressive	14
Present Perfect (1)	16
Present Perfect (2): **just, already, yet; for** and **since**	18
Present Perfect (3): **ever, this week,** etc.	20
Present Perfect Progressive	22
Past Perfect	24
Past Perfect Progressive	26
The future	28
Will and **shall**	30
Be going to	32
The verb **have**	34

Questions, negatives, and answers

Yes/no questions	36
Short answers	38
Question tags	40
So/Neither do I and I **think so**	42

Modal verbs

Permission: **can, may, could,** and **be allowed to**	44
Necessity: **have to** and **must**	46
Necessity: **must not, don't have to, don't need to**	48

Prepositions

In, **on**, and **at** (place)   96

In, **on**, and **at** (time)   98

Preposition + noun   100

Verbs with prepositions and adverbs

Prepositional verbs   102

Reported speech

Direct speech and reported speech   104

Conditionals and wish

Zero and First Conditionals (Real Conditionals)   106

First and Second Conditionals (Real and Unreal Conditionals)   108

Second and Third Conditionals (Unreal and Past Conditionals)   110

Review test

                                                                                112

Appendices

Appendix 1: Word formation   116

Appendix 2: The spelling of endings   118

Appendix 3: Punctuation   120

Appendix 4: Pronunciation   122

Appendix 5: Irregular verbs   125

Answer key

                                                                                127

Index

                                                                                136

Introduction

Canadian Grammar Spectrum is a series of books, each written at the appropriate level for you at each stage in your study of English. The series is intended for your use either in a classroom or when working independently on your own time.

The books are divided into two- to four-page units, each of which covers an important grammar topic. Each unit starts with an explanation of the grammar and this is followed by a set of practice exercises. A test at the end of each book gives the opportunity for more practice and enables you to assess how much you have learned. Answers to the exercises and the test are provided at the back of the book.

You may want to choose the order in which you study the grammar topics, perhaps going first to those giving you problems. (Topics are listed in the Contents page at the front of each book and in the Index at the back.) Alternatively, you may choose to start at the beginning of each book and work through to the end.

The emphasis throughout this book is on the meaning and use of the grammatical forms. The explanations of grammar are descriptions of how English works; they are a guide to help you understand, not rules to be memorized. It is often more effective to look at examples of English rather than to read statements about it, and the grammar explanations are supported by lots of examples of everyday conversational English.

Key to symbols

The symbol / (oblique stroke) between two words means that either word is possible. *I may/might go* means that *I may go* and *I might go* are both possible. In exercise questions this symbol is also used to separate words or phrases which are possible answers.

Parentheses ( ) around a word or phrase in the middle of a sentence mean that it can be left out. *There's (some) milk in the fridge* means that there are two possible sentences: *There's some milk in the fridge* and *There's milk in the fridge*.

The symbol ~ means that there is a change of speaker. In the example *How are you? ~ I'm fine, thanks*, the question and answer are spoken by different people.

The symbol ▶ in an exercise indicates that a sample answer is given.

Word classes: nouns, verbs, adjectives, etc.

1 Introduction

Look at the different kinds of word in this sentence.

Pronoun	Verb	Determiner	Adjective	Noun	Preposition	Noun	Adverb
I	*have*	*an*	*important*	*meeting*	*at*	*work*	*tomorrow,*

Linking word	Pronoun	Verb	Adverb	Adjective
so	*I*	*am*	*very*	*busy.*

2 What kind of word?

There are eight different kinds of word in English. They are called "word classes" or "parts of speech." Here are some examples from the conversations in the café.

1   Verb: **have, am, is, would, like, come, are, sitting, look**
2   Noun: **meeting, work, coffee, party, Saturday, Jessica, friends, corner**
3   Adjective: **important, busy, good, cheap**
4   Adverb: **tomorrow, very, really, here**
5   Preposition: **at, to, on, in**
6   Determiner: **an, this, our, the**
7   Pronoun: **I, it, you**
8   Linking word: **so, and**

3 Words in sentences

Some words can belong to different classes depending on how they are used in a sentence.

VERBS	NOUNS
*Can I **look** at your photos?*	*I like the **look** of that coat.*
*We **work** on Saturday morning.*	*I'll be at **work** tomorrow.*

Practice

A What kind of word? (2)

Read this paragraph and then decide which word class each underlined word belongs to. To help you decide, you can look back at the examples in 2.

Maurice didn't go to the café with the other students. Rachel told him they were going there, but he wanted to finish his work. Maurice isn't very sociable. He stays in his room and concentrates completely on his homework. He's an excellent student, but he doesn't have much fun.

► to   preposition   7   sociable   ....
► café   noun   8   in   ....
1 the   9   and   ....
2 told   10   completely ....
3 they   11   an   ....
4 there   12   excellent ....
5 he   13   but   ....
6 finish   14   fun   ....

B What kind of word? (2)

Read this paragraph and then write the words in the spaces below. Write the first three verbs under "Verb," and so on. Do not write the same word more than once.

Henri thinks Claire is wonderful. He loves her madly, and he dreams of marrying her, but unfortunately he is too old for her. Today they are at a café with their friends Sarah and Mark, so Henri can't get romantic with Claire. But he might buy her some flowers later.

Verb	Noun	Adjective	Adverb
thinks	Henri	....	....
....	....	....	....
....	....	....	....

Preposition	Determiner	Pronoun	Linking word
....	....	....	....
....	....	....	....
....	....	....	....

C Words in sentences (3)

Is the underlined word a verb, a noun, or an adjective?

► Shall we go for a walk?   noun ....
► Shall we walk into town?   verb ....
1 Laura wanted to talk to Rita.   ....
2 Laura wanted a talk with Rita.   ....
3 The windows aren't very clean.   ....
4 Doesn't anyone clean the windows?   ....
5 We went to a fabulous show in Vancouver. ....
6 Laura wanted to show Rita her photos. ....
7 Henri thought Claire looked beautiful. ....
8 A strange thought came into Siva's head. ....
9 Juan is tired now.   ....
10 Studying all night had tired Ben out. ....

Sentence structure: subject, verb, object, etc.

MIKE AND TERI ARE MOVING THEIR PIANO UPSTAIRS.
JEFF, MELANIE, AND DAVID ARE HELPING THEM.

I need a break.

It's giving me a backache.

My arms are aching.

This piano is heavy.

It's on my foot!

1 Sentence structure

The parts of a sentence are the subject, verb, object, complement, and adverbial. A statement begins with the subject and the verb. There are five main structures which we can use to make a simple statement.

1 | SUBJECT | VERB |
|---------|------|
| *My arms* | *are aching.* |
| *Something* | *happened.* |

2 | SUBJECT | VERB | OBJECT |
|---------|------|--------|
| *I* | *need* | *a break.* |
| *Five people* | *are moving* | *the piano.* |

The subject and object can be a pronoun (e.g. **I**) or a noun phrase (e.g. **the piano**).

3 | SUBJECT | VERB | COMPLEMENT |
|---------|------|------------|
| *This piano* | *is* | *heavy.* |
| *It* | *was* | *a big problem.* |

The complement can be an adjective (e.g. **heavy**) or a noun phrase (e.g. **a big problem**). The complement often comes after **be**. It can also come after **appear, become, get, feel, look, seem, stay,** or **sound**. For adjectives and word order see page 86, part 2.

4 | SUBJECT | VERB | ADVERBIAL |
|---------|------|-----------|
| *It* | *is* | *on my foot.* |
| *Their house* | *is* | *nearby.* |

An adverbial can be a prepositional phrase (e.g. **on my foot**) or an adverb (e.g. **nearby**).

5 | SUBJECT | VERB | OBJECT | OBJECT |
|---------|------|--------|--------|
| *It* | *'s giving* | *me* | *a backache.* |
| *David* | *bought* | *Melanie* | *a present.* |

We use two objects after verbs like **give** and **send** (see page 6).

2 Adverbials

We can add adverbials to all the five main structures.

*My arms are aching **terribly**.*   *I **really** need a rest.*

***Of course** this piano is heavy.*   ***Fortunately** their house is nearby.*

***To everyone's surprise**, David **actually** bought Melanie a present **yesterday**.*

Practice

A Parts of the sentence (1)

Angie and Kevin are on vacation. They have written a postcard to Tracy and Andy. Look at each underlined phrase and decide which part of the sentence it is: subject, verb, object, complement, or adverbial.

- ▶ We're having <u>a great time</u>.   object ....
- 1 <u>The weather</u> is fantastic.   ....
- 2 We really <u>enjoy</u> camping.   ....
- 3 It's <u>a lot of fun</u>.   ....
- 4 We're <u>on a farm</u>.   ....
- 5 We like <u>this place</u>.   ....
- 6 The scenery is <u>beautiful</u>.   ....

B Sentence structure (1)

After moving the piano, the five friends took a break and had some lemonade.
Look at this part of their conversation and then write the letters a)–e) in the correct place.

- a) David: That was a difficult job.
- b) Jeff: ~~I agree.~~
- c) Mike: I'm on my deathbed.
- d) David: Someone should give us a medal.
- e) Teri: I made some more lemonade.

- ▶ Subject + verb   b ....
- 1 Subject + verb + object   ....
- 2 Subject + verb + complement   ....
- 3 Subject + verb + adverbial   ....
- 4 Subject + verb + object + object   ....

C Word order (1)

Put the words in the correct order and write the statements.

- ▶ is / Melanie / very nice   Melanie is very nice. ....
- 1 football / likes / Jeff   ....
- 2 an accident / David / had   ....
- 3 moved / the piano / we   ....
- 4 a tall woman / Teri / is   ....
- 5 sat / on the floor / everyone   ....
- 6 gave / some help / Mike's friends / him   ....

D Adverbials (2)

These sentences are from a news report. Write down the two adverbials in each sentence.
Each adverbial is a prepositional phrase or an adverb.

- ▶ The premier opened a new arena in Winnipeg yesterday.   in Winnipeg .... yesterday ....
- 1 He also spoke with several young people.   ....
- 2 The arena was first planned in 2011.   ....
- 3 Naturally, the city council could not finance the project without help.   ....
- 4 Fortunately, they managed to obtain money from the province.   ....

Direct and indirect objects

1 Introduction

*Hudson gave **Alix some flowers**.* Here the verb **give** has two objects. **Alix** is the indirect object, the person receiving something. **Some flowers** is the direct object, the thing that someone gives.	*Hudson gave **some flowers to Alix**.* Here **give** has a direct object (**some flowers**) and a phrase with **to**. **To** comes before **Alix**, the person receiving something.

Here are some more examples of the two structures.

	INDIRECT OBJECT	DIRECT OBJECT		DIRECT OBJECT	PHRASE WITH TO/FOR
Jose gave	***Rachel***	***a book.***	*Jose gave*	***the book***	***to Rachel.***
I'll send	***my cousin***	***a postcard.***	*I'll send*	***a postcard***	***to my cousin.***
We bought	***all the children***	***ice cream***	*We bought*	***ice cream***	***for all the children.***

2 To or **for**?

We give something *to* someone, and we buy something *for* someone.

We can use **to** with these verbs: **bring, feed, give, hand, lend, offer, owe, pass, pay, post, promise, read, sell, send, show, take, teach, tell, throw, write**

> *Vicky paid the money **to** the cashier.* OR *Vicky paid the cashier the money.*
> *Let me read this news item **to** you.* OR *Let me read you this news item.*
> *We showed the photos **to** Nando.* OR *We showed Nando the photos.*

We can use **for** with these verbs: **book, bring, build, buy, choose, cook, fetch, find, get, leave, make, order, pick, reserve, save**

> *They found a spare ticket **for** me.* OR *They found me a spare ticket.*
> *I've saved a seat **for** you.* OR *I've saved you a seat.*
> *Marina is making a cake **for** David.* OR *Marina is making David a cake.*

3 Give + pronoun

Sometimes there is a pronoun and a noun after a verb such as **give**.
The pronoun usually comes before the noun.

Hudson likes Alix. He gave ***her some flowers***. We use **her** because Alix is mentioned earlier. **Her** comes before **some flowers**.	*Hudson bought some flowers. He gave* ***them to Alix***. We use **them** because the flowers are mentioned earlier. **Them** comes before **Alix**.

Practice

A Give (1)

Look at the birthday presents and write sentences about them.
Put one of these words at the end of each sentence: *necklace*, *scarf*, *sweater*, *tennis racquet*, *watch*.

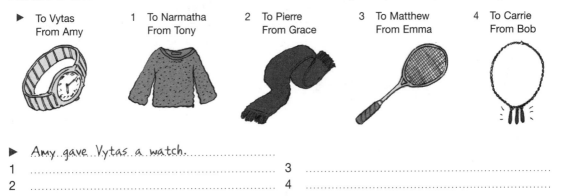

| ▶ To Vytas | 1 To Narmatha | 2 To Pierre | 3 To Matthew | 4 To Carrie |
| From Amy | From Tony | From Grace | From Emma | From Bob |

▶ Amy gave Vytas a watch. ....

1 ....   3 ....

2 ....   4 ....

B Indirect object or to? (1)

Write the information in one sentence. Put the underlined part at the end of the sentence.
Sometimes you need *to*.

▶ Daniel lent something to Vicky. It was <u>his calculator</u>. → Daniel lent Vicky his calculator.
▶ Mark sent a message. It was to <u>his boss</u>. → Mark sent a message to his boss.
1 Maddie sold her bike. <u>Her sister</u> bought it. → Maddie ....
2 Tom told the joke. He told <u>all his friends</u>. → Tom ....
3 Angelique gave <u>some help</u>. She helped her neighbour. → Angelique ....
4 Ilona wrote to her teacher. She wrote <u>a letter</u>. → Ilona ....

C To or for? (2)

Mark's boss at Zedco is Mr Prina. He is telling people to do things. Write *to* or *for*.

▶ Give these papers .to... my secretary.
▶ Could you make some coffee .for.. us?
1 Book a flight .... me, could you?
2 Can you mail this cheque .... the hotel?

3 Don't show these plans .... anyone.
4 Leave a message .... my secretary.
5 Get the file .... me, would you?
6 Write a memo .... all managers.

D Give + pronoun (3)

Complete each answer using the words in parentheses. Sometimes you need to use *to* or *for*.

▶ Gustav: Why is everyone laughing? (a funny story/us)
   Vicky: Daniel told .us. a. funny. story. ....
▶ Trevor: There's some fish left over. (it/the cat)
   Laura: I'll feed .it. to. the. cat. ....
1 Mark: What are you doing with those bottles? (them/the recycling bin)
   Sarah: I'm taking ....
2 Sean: How are things with you, Daniel? (a job/me)
   Daniel: Fine. Someone has offered ....
3 Brendan: What about those papers you found? (them/the police)
   Max: Oh, I handed ....
4 Kate: It's pouring rain—look. (my umbrella/you)
   Rachel: It's OK. I'll lend ....

Simple Present

Yes, I **like** this supermarket. I **think** it's very good. Yes, my husband **thinks** so, too. We always **shop** here. We **come** here every week. We **live** near the store, so it **doesn't take** long to get here.

1 Use

We use the Simple Present for

▶ thoughts and feelings: *I **think** so, I **like** it.*

▶ states, things staying the same, facts and things that are true for a long time: *We **live** near the store.*

▶ repeated actions: *We **come** here every week.*

and also

▶ in phrases like **I promise, I agree,** etc: *I **promise** I'll pay you back.*

▶ in a negative question with **why** to make a suggestion: *Why **don't** we **go** out?*

2 Positive forms

> I/you/we/they **get**
> he/she/it **gets**

In the Simple Present we use the verb without an s at the end.

*I usually **get** the lunch ready at one o'clock.*   *We always **do** our shopping at Foodmart.*
*Most children **like** ice cream.*   *You **know** the answer.*

But in the third person singular (after **he, she, it, your friend,** etc), the verb ends in -**s** or -**es**. For spelling rules see page 118.

*It **gets** busy on weekends.*   *My husband **thinks** so, too.*
*Sarah **catches** the early train.*   *She **travels** all over the world.*

3 Negatives and questions

NEGATIVE	QUESTION
I/you/we/they **do not get** OR **don't get**	**do** I/we/you/they **get?**
he/she/it **does not get** OR **doesn't get**	**does** he/she/it **get?**

We use a form of **do** in negatives and questions. We use **do** and **don't** except in the third person singular, where we use **does** and **doesn't.**

*We **don't live** far away.*   *He **doesn't want** to go shopping.*
***Do** you **live** here? ~ Yes, I do.*   *What **does** he **want?** ~ Money.*

We do not add -**s** to the verb in negatives and questions.

NOT ~~He doesn't gets~~ and NOT ~~Does he gets?~~

Practice

A Use (1)

Look at each <u>underlined</u> verb and describe what kind of meaning it expresses. Is it a thought, a feeling, a fact, or a repeated action?

▶ Matthew <u>loves</u> baseball.   a feeling

▶ Ahmed often <u>works</u> late at the office.   a repeated action

1 I <u>hate</u> reality shows.

2 We <u>play</u> hockey every Thursday.

3 The computer <u>belongs</u> to Emma.

4 These plates <u>cost</u> $20 each.

5 I <u>believe</u> it's the right thing to do.

6 I'm hungry. I <u>want</u> something to eat.

7 I usually <u>go</u> to work by bus.

8 It's OK. I <u>understand</u> your problem.

B Forms (2–3)

Complete the sentences by writing the verbs. Use the Simple Present. You have to decide if the verb is positive or negative.

▶ Marie is very sociable. She knows (know) lots of people.

▶ We've got plenty of chairs, thanks. We don't want (want) any more.

1 My friend is finding life in Quebec a bit difficult. He .... (speak) French.

2 Most students live close to the college, so they .... (walk) there.

3 My uniform is really dirty. This jersey .... (need) a good wash.

4 I have four cats and two dogs. I .... (love) animals.

5 Marcus doesn't need any pancakes. He .... (eat) breakfast.

6 What's the matter? You .... (look) very happy.

7 Don't try to ring the doorbell. It .... (work).

8 I hate voicemail. I just .... (like) having my voice recorded.

9 Gerard is good at badminton. He .... (win) every game.

10 We always travel by bus. We .... (own) a car.

C Forms (2–3)

Complete the conversation. Write the Simple Present forms.

Rita: (▶) Do you like (you/like) hockey, Antonio?

Antonio: (▶) I love (I/love) it. I'm a Habs fan. (1) .... (I/go) to all their home games. Nick usually (2) .... (come) with me. And (3) .... (we/travel) to some away games, too. Why (4) .... (you/not/come) to a game some time?

Rita: I'm afraid hockey (5) .... (not/make) sense to me—men chasing a puck. Why (6) .... (you/take) it so seriously?

Antonio: It's a wonderful game. (7) .... (I/love) it. The Canadiens are my whole life.

Rita: How much (8) .... (it/cost) to buy the tickets and pay for the travel?

Antonio: A lot. (9) .... (I/not/know) exactly how much. But (10) .... (that/not/matter) to me. (11) .... (I/not/want) to do anything else. (12) .... (that/annoy) you?

Rita: No, (13) .... (it/not/annoy) me. I just (14) .... (find) it a bit sad.

Present Progressive

1 Introduction

The Present Progressive shows that
we are in the middle of an action.

> Abdul? I'm at the station.
> **I'm waiting** for the train.
> Oh, I can hear it.
> It**'s coming** now.

JACLYN'S TRAIN IS LATE, SO SHE IS
CALLING ABDUL.

2 Form

The Present Progressive is the present tense of **be** + an **-ing** form.

POSITIVE

*I **am looking*** OR *I**'m looking***
*you/we/they **are looking*** OR *you/we/they**'re looking***
*he/she/it **is looking*** OR *he/she/it**'s looking***

NEGATIVE	QUESTION
*I**'m not looking***	*am I looking?*
*you/we/they **aren't looking*** OR *you/we/they**'re not looking***	*are you/we/they looking?*
*he/she/it **isn't looking*** OR *he/she/it**'s not looking***	*is he/she/it looking?*

---

*I**'m getting** lunch ready.*   *The train **is coming**—look.*
*We**'re looking** for a post office.*   *Rachel **isn't wearing** her new dress.*
*What **are** you **doing**?*   *Who **is** Candice **dancing** with?*

For rules about the spelling of the **-ing** form see page 118.

3 Use

We use the Present Progressive to say that we are in the middle of an action.
> *I**'m waiting** for the train.* (I'm at the station <u>now</u>.)
> *I**'m getting** lunch ready.* (I'm in the kitchen <u>now</u>.)

I'm waiting means that I am in the middle of a period of waiting. The wait is not yet over.

We can also use the Present Progressive when we are in the middle of something but not actually doing it
at the moment of speaking.
> *I should get back to the office. We**'re working** on a new project.*
> *I'm very busy these days. I**'m taking** a course at the college.*

We can use the Present Progressive when things are changing over a long period.
> *The number of cars on the road **is increasing**.*   *The earth **is** slowly **getting** warmer.*

Practice

A Form (2)

Look at the pictures and describe what people are doing.
Use these verbs: *carry, paint, play, ride, take*
Use these objects: *a bicycle, a package, a photo, a picture, basketball*

▶ He's riding a bicycle.

1 .... 3 ....

2 .... 4 ....

B Form (2)

Cecilia is in the student lounge at her college. Complete her conversation with Andrew.
Write a Present Progressive form of the verb.

Andrew: What (▶) are you doing? (you/do)

Cecilia: (▶) I'm writing (I/write) an email to a friend. He's a DJ. Marta and I
(1) .... (try) to organize a club night.

Andrew: That sounds a lot of work. How (2) .... (you/find) time for your
homework?

Cecilia: Well, as I said, Marta (3) .... (help) me.
(4) .... (we/do) all right. (5) ....
(we/not/spend) too much time on it. (6) .... (it/not/take) me away
from my homework—don't worry about that. Oh, sorry, (7) ....
(you/wait) for this seat?

Andrew: Yes, but there's no hurry.

Cecilia: (8) .... (I/finish) the last part of the email. I'm almost finished.

C Use (3)

What can you say in these situations? Add a sentence with the Present Progressive.

▶   A friend calls you in the middle of the hockey game.
Is it important? I'm watching the hockey game.

1   A friend is at your apartment and suggests going out, but you can see rain outside.
I don't want to go out now. Look, ...

2   A friend calls you at work.
Sorry, I can't talk now. ....

3   You want to get off the bus, but the man next to you is sitting on your coat.
Excuse me, ...

4   A friend wants to talk to you, but you have just started to write an important letter.
Can I talk to you later? ....

5   You have been sick, but you're better now than you were.
I'm OK now. ....

Simple Past

1 Introduction

It all **happened** very quickly. The car **came** straight out of the side road, and the van **went** into the back of it. The van driver **didn't have** a chance. It **was** the car driver's fault.

2 Positive forms

A regular past form ends in **-ed**.

>*It **happened** very quickly.*   *The van **crashed** into the car.*
>*I **mailed** the letter yesterday.*   *We once **owned** a kayak.*

For spelling rules, see page 118.

Some verbs have an irregular past form.

>*The car **came** out of a side road.*   *Carlos **sang** in the choir.*   *I **won** the game.*
>*I **had** breakfast at six.*   *The train **left** on time.*   *We **took** some photos.*

For a list of irregular verbs, see pages 125–26.

The Simple Past is the same in all persons, except in the past tense of **be**.

POSITIVE	
*I/he/she/it **was***	*I **was** sick last week.*
*you/we/they **were***	*Those samosas **were** spicy.*

3 Negatives and questions

NEGATIVE	QUESTION
*I/you/he/she/it/we/they **did not stop***	*did I/you/he/she/it/we/they **stop**?*
OR ***didn't stop***	

>*The car **did not stop**.*   *The driver **didn't look** to his right.*
>*What **did** you tell **the** police? ~ Nothing.*   ***Did** you **call** home? ~ Yes, I did.*

We do not use a past form such as **stopped** or **called** in negatives and questions.

>NOT *The car didn't stopped* and NOT *Did you called?*

We also use **was** and **were** in negatives and questions.

NEGATIVE	QUESTION
*I/he/she/it **was not** OR **wasn't***	*was I/he/she/it?*
*you/we/they **were not** OR **weren't***	*were you/we/they?*

>*I **wasn't** very well last week.*   *The gates **weren't** open.*
>*Where **was** your friend last night?*   ***Was** your steak good?*

4 Use

We use the Simple Past for something in the past which is finished.

>*Shauna **passed** her exam **last year**.*   *We **went** to the theatre **on Friday**.*   *Pierre Trudeau **died** in 2000.*
>*I **knew** what the problem **was**.*   *When **did** you **buy** this car? ~ About **three years ago**.*

A Positive forms (2)

What did Malin do on vacation last month? Look at her photos and use these words:
go out dancing, have a picnic, lie on the beach, play volleyball, swim in the ocean

▶   *She lay on the beach.*
1   3   ....
2   4   ....

B Positive forms (2)

Complete the newspaper story about a fire. Write the Simple Past forms of the verbs.

Two people (▶) .died.......... (die) in a fire on Robson Street, Vancouver, yesterday morning. They
(1)... (be) Herbert and Molly Chen, a couple in their seventies. The fire
(2) .... (start) at 3:20 a.m. A neighbour, Mr. Aziz, (3) .... (see)
the flames and (4) .... (call) the fire department. He also
(5) .... (try) to get into the house and rescue his neighbours, but the heat
(6) .... (be) too much. The fire department (7) .... (arrive)
in five minutes. Twenty firefighters (8) .... (fight) the fire and finally
(9) .... (bring) it under control. Two firefighters (10) .... (enter)
the burning building but (11) .... (find) the couple dead.

C Negatives and questions (3)

Complete the conversation. Write the Simple Past negatives and questions.

Shari: (▶) Did you have .... (you/have) a nice weekend in Toronto?
Marc: Yes, thanks. It was good. We walked around and then we saw a show.
           (1) .... (we/not/try) to do too much.
Shari: What sights (2) .... (you/see)?
Marc: We went to the Royal Ontario Museum. (3) .... (I/not/know)
           there was so much in there.
Shari: And what show (4) .... (you/go) to?
Marc: Oh, a musical. I forget the name. (5) .... (I/not/like) it.
Shari: That's too bad. And (6) .... (Sarah/enjoy) it?
Marc: No, not really. But we enjoyed the weekend. Sarah did some shopping, too, but
           (7) .... (I/not/want) to go shopping.

Past Progressive

1 Introduction

The Past Progressive shows that at a time in the past we were in the middle of an action.

> I had a wonderful dream last night. I **was sitting** in a park. The sun **was shining** and the birds **were singing**. Children **were playing** and **laughing**. It was very peaceful. I didn't want to wake up.

2 Form

The Past Progressive is the past tense of **be** + an **-ing** form.

POSITIVE

*I/he/she/it **was playing**
you/we/they **were playing***

NEGATIVE

*I/he/she/it **wasn't playing**
you/we/they **weren't playing***

QUESTION

***was** I/he/she/it **playing?**
were you/we/they **playing?***

> *Soft music **was playing**. People **were walking** in the park.*
> *I **wasn't dreaming**. I really was in New York City.*
> *Why did you give our secret away? What **were** you **thinking**?*
> ***Was** Mathieu already **waiting** for you when you got there?*

3 Use

Read this conversation.

Jehn: *I went to your house at about three yesterday afternoon, but you weren't in. I didn't know where you were.*

Manny: *Oh, I **was helping** Mike. We **were fixing** his car. It took ages. We **were working** on it all afternoon.*

Jehn: *It **was raining**. I hope you **weren't doing** it outside.*

Manny: *No, we were in the garage. So I didn't get wet. But I'm afraid I got oil all over my new jeans.*

Jehn: *Why **were** you **wearing** your new jeans to fix a car?*

Manny: *I don't know. I forgot I had them on.*

It was raining at three o'clock means that at three o'clock we were in the middle of a period of rain. The rain began before three and stopped some time after three. *We were working all afternoon* means that the action went on for the whole period. Manny is stressing the length of time that the work went on.

We use the progressive with actions. We do not normally use it with state verbs. For states we use the Simple Past.

> *I didn't know where you were.* NOT *I ~~wasn't knowing~~ ...*

Practice

A Form (2)

Today is January first, the start of a new year. Most people are feeling a bit tired.
What were they doing at midnight last night?
Use these verbs: *dance, drive, listen, watch, write*
Use these phrases after the verb: *an essay, his taxi, in the street, television, to a band*

▶ Claire was listening to a band.
1 Trevor and Laura ....
2 Vicky and Rachel ....
3 Jerome ....
4 Hector ....

B Form (2)

Complete the conversation. Write the Past Progressive forms.

Jessica: (▶) I was looking .... (I/look) for you, Kelly. I'm afraid I've broken this dish.
Kelly: Oh no! What (1) .... (you/do)?
Jessica: (2) .... (I/take) it into the kitchen. I bumped into Julie.
          (3) .... (she/come) out just as
          (4) .... (I/go) in.
Kelly: I expect it was your fault. (5) .... (you/not/look) where
          (6) .... (you/go).
Jessica: Sorry. I'll buy you another one as soon as I have some money.

C Use (3)

What can you say in these situations? Add a sentence with the Past Progressive
to show that an action lasted a long time.

▶ You had to work yesterday. The work went on all day.
  I was working all day yesterday.
1 You had to make phone calls. The calls went on all evening.
  ....
2 You had to wait in the rain. The wait lasted for half an hour.
  ....
3 You had to make sandwiches. This went on all afternoon.
  ....
4 You had to sit in a traffic jam. You were there for two hours.
  ....
5 Your neighbour played loud music. This went on all night.
  ....

Present Perfect (1)

1 Introduction

The aircraft **has landed**. They**'ve opened** the doors.

The Present Perfect tells us about the past and the present.
The aircraft has landed means that the aircraft is on the ground now.

2 Form

The Present Perfect is the present tense of **have** + a past participle.

POSITIVE

I/you/we/they **have washed** OR *I/you/we/they***'ve washed**
he/she/it **has washed** OR *he/she/it***'s washed**

NEGATIVE

I/you/we/they **haven't washed**
he/she/it **hasn't washed**

QUESTION

have *I/you/we/they* **washed**?
has *he/she/it* **washed**?

Regular past participles end in -**ed**, e.g. **washed, landed, finished**.
 We've washed the dishes. **Have** *you* **opened** *your letter?*
 The aircraft **has landed** *safely.* *How many goals* **has** *Sidney* **scored**?
 The students **haven't finished** *their test.*

3 Irregular forms

Some participles are irregular.
 I've **made** *a shopping list.* *We've* **sold** *our car.* *I've* **thought** *about it a lot.*
 Have you **written** *the letter?* *She hasn't* **drunk** *her coffee.*
For a list of irregular verbs see pages 125–26.

There is a Present Perfect of **be** and of **have**.
 The weather **has been** *awful.* *I've* **had** *a wonderful time, thank you.*

4 Use

When we use the Present Perfect, we are referring to things that happened in the past but that have a result in the present.
 We've **washed** *the dishes.* (They're clean <u>now</u>.) *The aircraft* **has landed**. (It's on the ground <u>now</u>.)
 We've **eaten** *all the eggs.* (There aren't any left.) *They've* **learned** *the words.* (They know the words.)
 You've **broken** *this watch.* (It isn't working.)

A Form (2)

Add a sentence. Use the Present Perfect.

▶ I'm tired. (I/walk/miles) ....I've walked miles...
1 Emma's computer is working now. (she/fix/it) ....
2 It's cooler in here now. (I/open/the window) ....
3 The visitors are here at last. (they/arrive) ....
4 Mohammad's car isn't blocking us in now. (he/move/it) ....
5 We haven't got any new movies. (we/watch/all these) ....

B Irregular forms (3)

Look at the pictures and describe what the people have done.
Use these verbs: *break*, *build*, *catch*, *see*, ~~win~~
Use these objects: *a movie*, *a fish*, *a house*, *his leg*, ~~the gold medal~~

▶ .....She's won the gold medal.......................
1 ....   3 ....
2 ....   4 ....

C Present Perfect (1–4)

Ali and Marie are painting their house. Write the verbs. Use the Present Perfect.

Marie: How is the painting going? (▶) ...Have you finished?.......... (you/finish)
Ali: No, I haven't. Painting the ceiling is really difficult, you know.
(1) .... (I/not/do) very much. And it looks just the same as before. This new paint (2) .... (not/make) any difference.
Marie: (3) .... (you/not/put) enough on.
Ali: (4) .... (I/hurt) my back. It feels sore.
Marie: Oh, you and your back. You mean (5) .... (you/have) enough of painting. Well, I'll do it. Where (6) .... (you/put) the brush?
Ali: I don't know. (7) .... (it/disappear).
(8) .... (I/look) for it, but I can't find it.
Marie: You're hopeless, aren't you? How much (9) .... (you/do) in here? Nothing! (10) .... (I/paint) two doors.
Ali: (11) .... (I/clean) all this old paint around the window. It looks much better now, doesn't it?
Marie: (12) .... (we/make) some progress, I suppose. Now, where (13) .... (that brush/go)?
Oh, (14) .... (you/leave) it on the ladder, look.

Present Perfect (2):
just, already, yet; for and since

I've **just heard** about the concert. **Have** you **bought** a ticket **yet**?

We're too late. They**'ve already sold** all the tickets.

Oh no!

DENISE SEES GIOVANNA OUTSIDE THE CONCERT HALL.

1 Just, already, and yet

We can use the Present Perfect with **just**, **already**, and **yet**.

Just means "a short time ago." Denise heard about the concert not long ago. **Already** means "sooner than expected." They sold the tickets very quickly. We use **yet** when we are expecting something to happen. Denise expects that Giovanna will buy a ticket.

Just and **already** come before the past participle (**heard, sold**). **Yet** comes at the end of a question or a negative sentence.

Here are some more examples.
> We**'ve just come** back from our vacation.
> I**'ve just had** an idea.
> It isn't a very good party. Most people **have already gone** home.
> My brother **has already crashed** his new car.
> It's eleven o'clock and you **haven't finished** breakfast **yet**.
> **Has** your course **started yet**?

2 For and since

We can use the Present Perfect with **for** and **since**.
> Courtney **has** only **had** that camera **for** three days.   Those people **have been** at the hotel **since** Friday.
> I**'ve felt** really tired **for** a whole week now.
> We**'ve lived** in Guelph **since** 2009. NOT ~~We live here since 2009.~~

Here something began in the past and has lasted up to the present time.

We use **for** to describe how long this period is (**for** three days). We use **since** to describe when the period began (**since** Friday).

We use **how long** in questions.
> **How long has** Courtney **had** that camera? ~ Since Thursday, I think.
> **How long have** Jacob and Julia **been** married? ~ Oh, for about three years.

We can also use the Present Perfect with **for** and **since** when something has stopped happening.
> I **haven't seen** Rachel **for** ages. She **hasn't visited** us **since** July.

Practice

A Just (1)

Write replies using the Present Perfect and *just*.

Use these past participles: *checked, eaten, made, remembered, called, cleaned*

▶ We must find out the address. ~ It's all right, I've just remembered it.

1 The kids' room looks neat. ~ Yes, they've

2 Is Daniel making some coffee? ~ It's ready.

3 What happened to that chocolate? ~ Sorry,

4 Did Camilla get all the answers right? ~ Yes,

5 Have you told your sister? ~ Yes, I've

B Just, already, and yet (1)

Complete the dialogue. Use the Present Perfect with *just*, *already*, and *yet*.

Toni: (▶) You haven't done your project yet (you/not do/your project/yet), I suppose.

Stanley: No, I haven't. (1) ....

          (I/not/start/it/yet).

Toni: (2) .... (I/just/see/Andrew), and he says

          (3) .... (he/already/finish) about half of his project.

Stanley: Well, he works too hard.

Toni: (4) ....

          (I/not/finish/my outline/yet).

Stanley: (5) .... (you/already/begin) to worry about it, haven't you?

          Take it easy. There's plenty of time.

Toni: (6) .... (we/already/spend) too long thinking about it.

          (7) .... (I/not/do/any real work/yet)

          and (8) .... (I/just/realize) that there are only four

          weeks to the end of the semester.

Stanley: OK. (9) .... (I/just/decide) to start next week. Well,

          maybe.

C For and since (2)

Felix is a very hard-working student. It's midnight and he is still working at his computer.

Write sentences with the Present Perfect and *for* or *since*.

▶	be/at his computer/six hours	He's been at his computer for six hours.
1	not/have/any fun/a long time	....
2	have/a cold/a week	....
3	not/see/his friends/weeks	....
4	not/play/any sports/last year	....
5	be/busy with his classes/months	....

D For and since (2)

Complete the sentences.

▶ You ought to wash the car. You haven't washed it for .... ages.

▶ I'd better have a shower. I haven't had one since .... Thursday.

1 I think I'll call my girlfriend. I haven't .... the weekend.

2 We're going to see some old friends. We haven't .... five years.

3 Let's watch a movie. We haven't .... quite a while.

4 We could have a barbecue. We haven't .... last summer.

5 Shall we play tennis? We haven't .... our vacation.

Present Perfect (3): ever, this week, etc.

1 Gone to or been to?

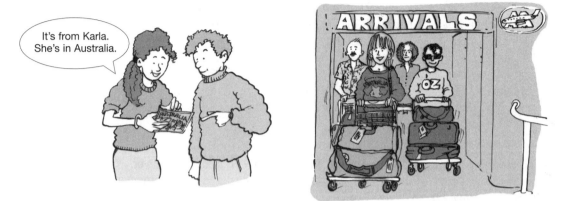

> It's from Karla. She's in Australia.

ARRIVALS

*Karla has **gone to** Australia.*
Gone there means that she is still there.

*Karla has **been to** Australia.*
Been there means that the visit is over.

2 Ever and never

Bryan: *Where have you been this time, Brenda?*
Brenda: *I've just come back from Mexico.*
Bryan: *You get around, don't you? **I've never been** to Mexico. Was it good?*
Brenda: *It was OK. Not as good as Cuba. I might go to Brazil next time. **Have** you **ever been** there?*
Bryan: *No, I haven't.*

We can use **ever** and **never** with the Present Perfect. We use **ever** in questions. In *Have you ever been to Brazil?* the word **ever** means "in your whole life up to the present time." **Never** means "not ever."

Here are some more examples.
> ***Have** you **ever played** lacrosse? ~ No, **never**.*   ***Has** Helena **ever had** any fun? ~ I don't think so.*
> *I've **never ridden** a snowmobile in my life.*   *You've **never given** me flowers before.*
> *This is the most expensive hotel we've **ever stayed** in.*

3 First time, second time, etc.

After **It's/This is the first/second time**, we use the Present Perfect.
> *This is the **first time** we've been to Nova Scotia, so it's all new to us.*
> *This is the **second time** Zaira **has forgotten** to give me a message.*
> *I love this movie. I think it's the **fourth time** I've seen it.*

4 Today, this week, etc.

We use the Present Perfect with **today** and phrases with **this**, e.g. **this morning, this week, this year**.
> *We've **done** quite a lot of work **today**.*
> *I **haven't watched** any television so far **this week**.*
> ***Have** you **had** a day off **this month**? ~ No, not yet.*
This year is the period which began in January and has lasted up to the present time.

Practice

A Gone to or been to? (1)

Complete the conversation. Write *gone* or *been*.

Anna: Hi. Where's Dina?
Patty: She's (▶) *gone* .... to the store to get something for dinner.
Anna: But I have some chicken for tonight. I've just (1) .... to the new grocery store on Queen Street.
Natasha: I haven't (2) .... to that one yet.
Patty: Where's Jessica? Isn't she here?
Anna: No, she's (3) .... to Coquitlam. She'll be back tomorrow.

B Ever and never (2)

Write the questions and answers. Use the information in parentheses.

▶ Matthew: (sailing?) *Have you ever been sailing?*
   Natasha: (no, windsurfing) *No, I've never been sailing, but I've been windsurfing.*
1 Laura: (San Francisco?) ....
   Mark: (no, Los Angeles) .... ,
   but ....
2 Tom: (basketball?) ....
   Trevor: (no, volleyball) .... ,
   but ....
3 Daniel: (*Hamlet*?) ....
   Vicky: (no, *Macbeth*) .... ,
   but ....

C First time, second time, etc. (3)

What would you say in these situations? Use *time* and the Present Perfect.

▶ You are watching a rugby game. You have never seen one before.
  This is the first time I've seen a rugby game.
1 You lost your debit card. It has happened once before.
  This is ....
2 The washing machine has broken down. This has happened twice before.
  ....
3 You are in Costa Rica for the first time in your life.
  ....
4 You are staying in a hotel where you once stayed before.
  ....
5 You have missed the bus. You've done the same thing about four times before.
  ....

D Today, this week, etc. (4)

Complete the sentences. Use the Present Perfect.

▶ Mark buys a newspaper most mornings, but *he hasn't bought one this morning.*
1 I see Janis most days, but ....
2 We go to the club most weekends, but ....
3 We usually have a party every semester, but ....
4 Someone usually calls in the evening, but no one ....

Present Perfect Progressive

1 Introduction

We use the Present Perfect Progressive for an action (*waiting*). The action happens over a period of time (*for twenty minutes*). Here the period lasts up to the present—they are still waiting now.

2 Form

The Present Perfect Progressive is the present tense of **have** + **been** + an **-ing** form.

POSITIVE
I/you/we/they **have been waiting** OR I/you/we/they**'ve been waiting** he/she/it **has been waiting** OR he/she/it**'s been waiting**

NEGATIVE	QUESTION
I/you/we/they **haven't been waiting** he/she/it **hasn't been waiting**	**have** I/you/we/they **been waiting?** **has** he/she/it **been waiting?**

We've been standing here forever.   *It has been snowing all day.*
Have you been waiting long?   *Our team hasn't been doing very well lately.*

3 Use

We use the Present Perfect Progressive for an action over a period of time leading up to the present (see 1). In these examples the action is still going on.

We've been waiting here for twenty minutes. (We're still waiting <u>now</u>.)
Listen. That burglar alarm has been ringing since eight o'clock this morning.

We must use the perfect in these situations.

NOT ~~We wait here for twenty minutes~~ OR ~~We're waiting here for twenty minutes.~~

We can use the Present Perfect Progressive to talk about repeated actions up to now.

Sarita has been playing the piano since she was four.

We can also use it to talk about an action which ends just before the present.

I've been swimming. That's why my hair is wet.

4 For, since, how long, and recently

We can use the Present Perfect Progressive with **for** and **since**.

My sister has been staying with me for three weeks now.
You've been playing on that computer since seven o'clock.

We use **how long** in questions.

How long have you been waiting?

Note also **recently** and **lately**. These both mean "in the last few days or weeks."

I haven't been feeling very well recently.   *What have you been doing lately?*

A Form (2)

Write the verbs. Use the Present Perfect Progressive.

Kim: Sorry I'm late.

Suki: It's OK. (▶) .I. haven't. been. waiting...... (I/not/wait) long.

What (1) .... (you/do)?

Kim: I've been with Mrs Noori. (2) .... (she/help) me with my English.

Suki: Your English is very good. I don't think you need lessons.

How long (3) .... (you/study) English?

Kim: Um, eight years now. But my accent wasn't so good before I came to Canada.

(4) .... (I/try) to improve it.

I think (5) .... (it/get) better lately.

Suki: Your accent is fine, Kim. Honestly.

B Use (3)

Describe what these people have been doing. Use these verbs: *argue, cook, drive, wait, work*

▶ Steve is tired because ...he's. been. working........... all day.

1 Francisco and Miranda are upset because ....

2 David is hot because ....

3 Sven feels very stiff because .... all day.

4 Chris is annoyed. .... a long time for Claire.

C Use (3–4)

What could you say in these situations? Write sentences with the Present Perfect Progressive and a phrase with *for*. Use these verbs: *play, read, swim, talk, travel, work*

▶ A movie is on. It began two hours ago, and it hasn't finished yet.

.The. movie. has. been. playing. for. two. hours...............................

1 Matthew went into the water an hour ago. He doesn't want to come out yet.

....

2 Your friends started their trip around the world three months ago. They've gone about halfway now.

....

3 Antonello got to the office early this morning. Ten hours later he's still there.

....

4 Celine called Rita forty minutes ago, and they're still on the phone.

....

5 Travis is reading an interesting book. He started it a long time ago.

....

Past Perfect

1 Introduction

IN THE CANTEEN AT WORK, DEREK IS TELLING A COLLEAGUE ABOUT THE AWFUL DAY HE HAD YESTERDAY.

*I felt really tired when I took the train to work yesterday because Sarah and I **had been** to a party the evening before. We **hadn't gone** to bed until after one. I **hadn't been** on the train long when I had a bit of a shock. I suddenly realized that I**'d left** my wallet at home. Then I began to wonder. **Had I left** it in the office the day before? I just couldn't remember. I wanted to go back to bed. I felt awful.*

The situation is in the past (*I **took** the train ... I **felt** tired ...*). When we talk about things <u>before</u> this past time, we use the Past Perfect.

> *Sarah and I **had been** to a party the evening before.*
> *I**'d left** my wallet at home.*

We are looking back from the situation of the train journey to the earlier actions—going to a party and leaving home without the wallet.

Here are some more examples of the Past Perfect.

*It was six o'clock. Most of the stores **had** just **closed**.*
*I went to the box office at lunch time, but they **had** already **sold** all the tickets.*
*By 1949 all of the provinces **had joined** Canada.*

As well as actions, we can use the Past Perfect to talk about states.

*I felt better by the summer, but the doctor warned me not to do too much. I**'d been** very sick.*
*The news came as no surprise to me. I**'d known** for some time that the factory was likely to close.*

2 Form

The Past Perfect is **had** + a past participle.

*He **had enjoyed** the party.* OR *He**'d enjoyed** the party.*
*They **hadn't gone** to bed until late.   Where **had** he **put** his wallet?*

For irregular past participles see pages 125–26.

3 Present Perfect and Past Perfect

Compare these examples.

PRESENT PERFECT (before <u>now</u>)	PAST PERFECT (before <u>then</u>)
*My wallet isn't here. I'**ve left** it behind.*	*My wallet wasn't there. I'**d left** it behind.*
*The game is over. The Canucks **have won**.*	*The game was over. The Canucks **had won**.*
*That man looks familiar. I'**ve seen** him somewhere before.*	*The man looked familiar. I'**d seen** him somewhere before.*

Practice

A Past Perfect (1)

Read about each situation and then check the correct answer.

▶ Two men delivered the sofa. I had already paid for it.
Which came first, a) ☐ the delivery, or b) ✓ the payment?

1 The waiter brought our drinks. We'd already had our soup.
Which came first, a) ☐ the drinks, or b) ☐ the soup?

2 I'd seen the movie, so I read the book.
Did I first a) ☐ see the movie, or b) ☐ read the book?

3 The show had ended, so I turned off the TV.
Did I turn off the TV a) ☐ after, or b) ☐ before the show ended?

4 I had an invitation to the party, but I'd planned a trip to Algonquin Park.
Which came first, a) ☐ the invitation, or b) ☐ the plans for the trip?

B Past Perfect (1–2)

Add a sentence with the Past Perfect using the notes.

▶ Arlene looked very suntanned when I saw her last week.
She'd just gone on vacation. (just / go on vacation)

1 We rushed to the station, but we were too late.
.... (the train/just/leave)

2 I didn't have an umbrella, but that didn't matter.
.... (the rain/stop)

3 When I got to the concert hall, they wouldn't let me in.
.... (forget/my ticket)

4 Someone got the licence plate of the car the burglars used.
.... (steal/it/a week before)

5 I was really happy to see Leigh again yesterday.
.... (not see/her/for months)

6 Luckily the apartment didn't look too bad when my parents stopped by.
.... (just/clean/it)

7 The boss invited me to lunch yesterday, but I had to refuse the invitation.
.... (already/eat/my sandwiches)

C Present Perfect and Past Perfect (3)

Write the verbs in the Present Perfect (*have done*) or Past Perfect (*had done*).

▶ It isn't raining now. It _has stopped_ (stop) at last.

▶ We had no car at that time. We _'d sold_ (sell) our old one.

1 The park looked awful. People .... (leave) litter everywhere.

2 You can have that newspaper. I .... (read) it.

3 There's no more cheese. We .... (eat) it all, I'm afraid.

4 There was no sign of a taxi, although I .... (order) one half an hour before.

5 This bill isn't right. They .... (make) a mistake.

6 I spoke to Kendra at lunch time. Someone .... (tell) her the news earlier.

7 I was really tired last night. I .... (have) a hard day.

8 Don't you want to see this show? It .... (start).

9 It'll get warm in here soon. I .... (turn) the heat on.

10 At last the committee was ready to announce its decision. The members ....
(make) up their minds.

Past Perfect Progressive

1 Introduction

I fell down the steps here and broke my leg. I'd taken a bus into town, and **I'd been swimming** in the pool here.

Javier is talking about a situation in the past (*I fell and broke* my leg). When we look back to something *before* this past time, we use the Past Perfect (see page 24) or the Past Perfect Progressive.

Past Perfect: *I **had taken** a bus into town.*
Past Perfect Progressive: *I **had been swimming** in the pool.*

We use the Past Perfect Progressive for an action which happened over a period of time. The swimming went on for some time before Javier broke his leg.

2 Form

The Past Perfect Progressive is **had been** + an -ing form.
> *I **had been waiting** for hours.* OR *I'**d been waiting** for hours.*
> *I **had not been paying** attention.* OR *I **hadn't been paying** attention.*
> *Was the ground wet?* **Had** *it* **been raining**?

3 I had been doing or I had done?

Compare the Past Perfect and the Past Perfect Progressive.

OVER A PERIOD (**had been doing**)	COMPLETE (**had done**)
*I found the calculator. I'**d been looking** for it forever.*	*I finally bought a new calculator. I'**d looked** everywhere for the old one.*
*Vanessa felt tired because she'**d been working** all day.*	*Vanessa felt pleased because she'**d done** so much work.*
We are thinking of Vanessa's working continuing as she got tired.	We are thinking of Vanessa's work as complete.
We normally use the Progressive form with a phrase saying *how long*.	We normally use the Past Perfect form with a phrase saying *how much/many*.
*When the company went bankrupt, it **had been losing** money for months.*	*When the company went bankrupt, it **had lost** over a million dollars.*
We do not normally use the Past Perfect Progressive for states.	We also use the Past Perfect for states.
NOT *He had been seeming unwell.*	*The old man **had seemed** unwell for some time before he died.*

4 Comparison with other progressive forms

Compare the *Present* Perfect Progressive (**has/have been doing**) and the *Past* Perfect Progressive (**had been doing**).
> *Sun looks very upset. I think she'**s been crying**.*
> *Sun looked very upset. I thought she'**d been crying**.*

Compare the Past Progressive (**was doing**) and the Past Perfect Progressive (**had been doing**).
> *When I called, Nadine **was having** a piano lesson.* (I called *during* the lesson.)
> *When I called, Nadine **had been having** a piano lesson.* (I called *after* the lesson.)

Practice

A Form (2)

Complete the conversation. Write the Past Perfect Progressive of the verbs.

June: How was your job interview?

Bhairavi: Awful. I felt so nervous. (▶) ......<u>I'd been worrying</u>. (I/worry) about it all week. And I was tired because (1) .... (I/work) on my project the night before.

(2) .... (I/not look) forward to the interview at all.

June: So what happened?

Bhairavi: The woman interviewing me was half an hour late because

(3) .... (she/deal) with an unexpected problem, she said.

(4) .... (I/wait) for a long time, and I got even more nervous.

June: How did the interview go?

Bhairavi: Well, I tried to sound confident. (5) .... (I/read) a book that said that's what you have to do in job interviews. But I don't know if I gave the right answers.

B Form and use (1–2)

Add a sentence with the Past Perfect Progressive to explain each thing that happened. Look at the pictures to find the reasons.

▶ lie/in the sun   1 cry   2 drive/too fast   3 play/with matches   4 stand/under a tree

▶ Therese got burnt. <u>She had been lying in the sun.</u> ....

1 Larissa looked upset. ....

2 Gobi was stopped by the police. ....

3 The children started a fire. ....

4 A young man was struck by lightning. ....

C Comparison with other forms (3–4)

Write the correct form of the verbs.

▶ Krishna could hear shouts from the apartment next door. His neighbours <u>were arguing</u>............ (argue) again.

1 Muna went into the living room. It was empty, but the television was still on. Someone .... (watch) it.

2 I .... (play) tennis, so I took a shower. I was annoyed because I .... (not win) a single game.

3 The walkers finally arrived at their destination. They .... (walk) all day, and they certainly needed a rest. They .... (walk) fifty kilometres.

4 When I saw Nick last week, he said he .... (stop) smoking. But when I saw him two days later, he .... (smoke) a cigarette. He looked ashamed.

5 I really should go to the dentist. One of my teeth .... (ache) for weeks.

6 When Karen arrived at Jack's place, he .... (lie) on the sofa reading a detective novel. He .... (buy) it at the second-hand bookstore, and he .... (read) it for most of the afternoon.

The future

1 Present, past, and future

Read this paragraph from Khadisha's letter to her aunt and uncle.

This is my last year at university, so I'll be graduating in June. And I've already got a job! In September I'm starting work at a bank in Montreal. So I'll be free for most of the summer. I'm going to spend six weeks travelling around the country. My friend Esther is coming with me. (She finishes university at the same time as me.) We're really looking forward to the trip. We might go to the States, too. Esther has friends in New York.

When we talk about the present or the past, we use verb forms to say what *is happening* now, what *happened* yesterday, and so on.

*Esther **has** friends in New York.*

We know about things in the present and in the past because they are already real. But talking about the future is more of a problem. There is no single form in English that we can always use for the future. There are many different ways of talking about the future, depending on how we see a future event. It may be something that is fairly sure to happen, but on the other hand it may be just a plan or an intention, or it may be something that you think will happen but you can't be sure about.

2 Verb forms used for the future

Here are some examples of verb forms used to express the future.

Be going to	*I'm going to spend six weeks travelling around the country.* (an intention)
Will	*I'll be free for most of the summer.* (neutral future)
Present Progressive	*I'm starting work in September.* (an arrangement)
Simple Present	*She finishes university at the same time.* (a timetable)
Will be doing	*I'll be graduating in June.* (in the course of events)

Very often there is more than one possible form that could be used.

She'll finish university in June.   *She finishes university in June.*
She's finishing university in June.   *She'll be finishing university in June.*

Khadisha could use any of these in her letter.

3 Will

We often use **will** as a neutral way of expressing the future, but it is not "the future tense."
It is only one of the forms we can use. In some situations **will** is not the right word.

After university I'm going to travel around the country.

Here Khadisha is saying what she intends to do in the future. We cannot use **will** here.

4 Being sure and unsure

We cannot always be sure about the future. To show that we are unsure we can use **might** or **could**.

*We **might** go to the States.   It **could** snow soon.*

To show how sure or unsure we are, we often use phrases like **I'm sure**, **definitely**, **I expect**, **I (don't) think**, and **probably**.

*__I'm sure__ it'll be all right.   We're **definitely** going to be at the meeting.*
*__I expect__ that everyone will be going home.   Kristina will **probably** be late.*
__I think__ I'm going to sneeze.   __I don't think__ Philippa's coming tonight.

A Present, past, and future (1–2)

Darcy has received a letter from a friend of hers who is in a retail training program.
Find the sentences which refer to the future and write them below.

I'm really enjoying my work at the store. I'm learning lots about the job. Soon they're moving me to another store—in Victoria. They told me about it last week. I'll be leaving here at the end of the month. I feel a bit sad about that. Luckily, they'll find an apartment for me.

The time is going by very quickly. I've been here three months. The training program finishes next summer. I like the work, and I want to stay with the company. They'll decide about that next year. I'm just hoping for the best.

▶ *Soon they're moving me to another store—in Victoria.*

1 ....

2 ....

3 ....

4 ....

B Present and future (1–4)

Decide whether the second sentence is about the present or the future.
Look at the phrases of time such as *at the moment* and *on Friday*.

▶ I'm busy. I'm cooking a meal at the moment.   *present*
1 I'm nervous. I'm cooking for ten people on Friday.   ....
2 I don't want to go out. I might watch a movie later.   ....
3 There's a football game on TV tonight. I might watch it.   ....
4 We're off at last. We arrive in Winnipeg at seven.   ....
5 This train is never on time. We always arrive late.   ....

C Present and future (1–4)

Read each pair of sentences and then answer the question about them.

▶ a) I'll see you on Thursday.
  b) I saw you on Thursday.
  Which sentence is about the future? *a*
1 a) I'm going to Edmonton. I'm waiting for a bus.
  b) I'm going to take a bus to Edmonton.
  Which is spoken during the trip? ....
2 a) We'll know the results of the tests next week.
  b) We might know the results of the tests next week.
  Which sentence is more certain? ....
3 a) I'm taking two courses this fall.
  b) I'm doing some homework at the moment.
  In which sentence has the action already started? ....
4 a) What time do we arrive in Stratford?
  b) What time will we arrive in Stratford?
  Which question is more likely if you are travelling by car? ....
5 a) I'm eating at the Thai restaurant tonight.
  b) I'll eat at the Thai restaurant tonight.
  Which would you say if you've booked a table? ....

Will and shall

The world leaders **will arrive** here tomorrow. They **will have** plenty to talk about, but they **won't be** here for long – only 24 hours. You**'ll hear** live reports every hour.

WORLD SUMMIT

1 Will for the future

We use **will** to say what we know or think about the future. **Will** here has a neutral meaning. It does *not* express the idea that we have already decided to do something or that we are planning something.

2 Will for instant decisions

We also use **will** for an instant decision, when we decide on something or agree to do it more or less at the moment of speaking.

> *I'm thirsty. I think I'll **drink** some water.*
> NOT *I drink some water.*
> *You've left your computer on. ~ Oh, I'll **go** and turn it off.*
> *We should celebrate. I know, we'll **have** a party.*
> *I don't think I'll **do** any work tonight. I'm too tired.*

We also use it to order things.

> *I'll **have** the ham salad, please.*

We also use **will** in offers and invitations.

Offer: *I'll **peel** the potatoes. ~ Oh, thank you.*
Invitation: **Will** *you **come** to lunch? ~ Yes, thank you. I'd love to.*
Promise: *I'll **pay** you back next week.*

3 The form of will

The form is **will** or **'ll** + infinitive.

> *Vancouver **will have** rain tomorrow.*   *You'll **be** late if you don't hurry.*
> ***Will** you **be** at home this evening?*   *The world **will end** in the year 2050.*

The negative is **will not** or **won't** + infinitive.

> *The cost **will not be** more than $50.*   *I **won't have** time for lunch.*

4 Shall

Shall is sometimes used in the same way as **will**. It is formal and not very common.
We can use **shall** for the future, but only in the first person, after I or **we**.

> *I **will be**/I **shall be** on vacation in August.*
> *We **will know**/We **shall know** the results soon.*
> But NOT *Everyone shall know the results soon.*

We can use **shall** in offers and suggestions.

Offer: ***Shall** I **pack** up your shopping for you? ~ Oh, thank you.*
Suggestion: ***Shall** we all **go** out together? ~ Good idea.*

Practice

A Will for the future and for instant decisions (1–2)

Read the conversations. Which replies are statements about the future and which are instant decisions?

▶ What would you like? ~ I'll have an orange juice, please. _decision_ ....

1 Shall we go out tonight? ~ I'll be too tired, I think. ....
2 We've lost a tennis ball. ~ I'll help you look for it. ....
3 I'm worried about the test. ~ Oh, you'll be all right. ....
4 I don't have a ride. ~ Oh, we'll give you a lift. ....
5 I need to fix this shelf some time. ~ We'll be dead before then ....

B Instant decisions (2)

Write what your decision is in these situations, or what you offer to do.
Use these verbs: *answer, carry, have, mail, ~~shut~~*

▶ You and your friend have come into the room. The window is open, and it is cold.
  I'll shut the window. ....

1 The phone is ringing. You are the nearest person to it.

  ....

2 The choice on the menu is fish or chicken. You hate fish.

  ....

3 You are meeting a friend at the train station. He has two suitcases. There's a bag, too.

  ....

4 Your friend has written a letter. You are going to walk into town past the post office.

  ....

C Will and won't for the future (3)

Use the notes to write about what will happen next weekend.

▶ it/be/warm/tomorrow   _It will be warm tomorrow._ ....
1 Josh/watch/the game   ....
2 Linda's party/be/fun   ....
3 Claude/not put up/the shelves ....
4 Gicela/be/annoyed   ....
5 Alejandro/study/all weekend ....
6 Heather/not do/any work   ....

D Will and shall (1, 4)

Complete the conversation. Write *will* or *shall*.

Ricardo: What (▶) _shall_............... we do today?
Alison: It would be nice to go out somewhere. The forecast says temperatures
         (1) .... rise to thirty degrees.
Kim: (2) .... we go for a walk?
Ricardo: That sounds a bit boring. What about the beach? We could take a bus.
Kim: How much (3) .... it cost? I don't have very much money.
Alison: It isn't far. It doesn't cost much.
Kim: Everywhere (4) .... be so crowded today because it's a holiday.
         The trip (5) .... take forever.
Ricardo: Come on, Alison. (6) .... we leave Kim behind if she's going to
         be so cranky?

Be going to

1 Intentions

I think the cat is stuck on the roof. **I'm going to climb** up and have a look.

Be careful, David.

We use **be going to** to talk about something we have decided to do (an intention). David intends to climb up the ladder.

Here are some more examples.

I'm going to watch the next show.
Emil is going to do an experiment this afternoon.
John and Jason are going to spend six weeks in Chile.

We can use **I'm not going to** for a refusal.

I'm sorry, but I'm not going to walk two kilometres in the rain.
(= I don't want to/I'm not willing to walk.)

The Present Progressive can have a very similar meaning to **be going to**. We can often use either form.

I'm going to visit my friend on the weekend.
I'm visiting my friend on the weekend.

We do not use **will** here.

We can use **be going to** with the verb **go** (*We're going to go out tonight*), but the Present Progressive is more common.

We're going out tonight.

2 Form

We use the present tense of **be** + **going to** + a verb.

They're going to move next month.   *Jared is going to play baseball.*
Selma isn't going to have any lunch.   *We aren't going to complain.*
Is Daniel going to apply for the job? ~ I think he is.
When are you going to pay this bill? ~ I don't know. I can't right now.

In informal speech "going to" is often pronounced /ɡənə/. You may see it written as *gonna*, but note that this is *not* proper English.

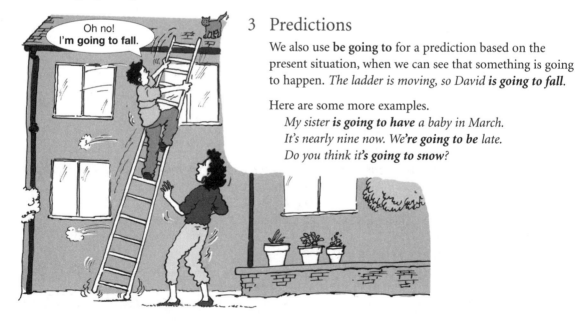

Oh no!
I'm going to fall.

3 Predictions

We also use **be going to** for a prediction based on the present situation, when we can see that something is going to happen. *The ladder is moving, so David is going to fall*.

Here are some more examples.

My sister is going to have a baby in March.
It's nearly nine now. We're going to be late.
Do you think it's going to snow?

Practice

A Intentions (1–2)

Look at the pictures and describe what is going to happen.
Use these verbs: *answer, catch, take, hit, light*
Use these objects: *the ball, a bath, a bus, the firework, the phone*

▶ They're going to take a bath. ....

1 ....

2 ....

3 ....

4 ....

B Form (2)

Write the verbs with *be going to*.

Ava: What are you doing with that camera?

Jordan: (▶) I'm going to take .... (I/take) it to work. (1) .... (I/lend)
it to Phil. (2) .... (he/take) a few photos with it.

Ava: Why can't he buy his own camera?

Jordan: He's got one, but it isn't working properly. (3) .... (it/be)
a while before he can get it repaired.

Ava: Well, how long (4) .... (he/keep) ours? When
(5) .... (we/get) it back?

Jordan: (6) .... (he/have) it over the weekend.
(7) .... (we/get) it back on Monday.

Ava: Well, I hope (8) .... (it/not/get) damaged.

C Predictions (2–3)

What would you say in these situations? Use these words: *be sick, crash, get wet, lose, not stop, ~~rain~~*

▶ The sky is full of dark clouds.
It's going to rain. ....

1 Now it's starting to rain. There's nowhere to go for shelter, and you don't have an umbrella.
....

2 You feel awful. There's a terrible feeling in your stomach.
....

3 You are playing Scrabble. The game is nearly over and you are 100 points behind.
....

4 You can see a plane coming down. It's out of control and falling to the ground.
....

5 You are waiting for a train. There's one coming, but you don't know if it's the one you want.
It's travelling very fast.
....

The verb **have**

1 **Have** and **have got**

Look at these examples.

HAVE	HAVE GOT
We **have** three cats.	We**'ve got** three cats.
Maya **has** toothache.	Riley **has got** blue eyes.
Cole **doesn't have** a car.	I **haven't got** any money.
Do you **have** the address?	**Have** you **got** a ticket?

Here **have** and **have got** mean the same thing. We can normally use either form. But **have** is more common.

2 Forms

	PRESENT TENSE	
	have	have got
POSITIVE	I/you/we/they **have**	I/you/we/they **have got** OR I/you/we/they**'ve got**
	He/she/it **has**	He/she/it **has got** OR He/she/it**'s got**
NEGATIVE	I/you/we/they **don't have**	I/you/we/they **haven't got**
	He/she/it **doesn't have**	He/she/it **hasn't got**
QUESTION	**Do** I/you/we/they **have**?	**Have** I/you/we/they **got**?
	Does he/she/it **have**?	**Has** he/she/it **got**?
	PAST TENSE	
POSITIVE	I/you/he/she/it/we/they **had**	
NEGATIVE	I/you/he/she/it/we/they **didn't have**	
QUESTION	**Did** I/you/he/she/it/we/they **have**?	

We do not often use **had got** in the past tense.

Caleb **had** several jobs to do.   We **didn't have** time to stop.   Why **did** you **have** that funny hat on?

3 The action verb **have**

Here are some examples of **have** as an action verb.

Ming **has** lunch around one.   I **have** cereal every morning.
The children **had** an orange ball.   We **had** a wonderful vacation.

Have expresses an action. *Ming has lunch* means that she eats lunch.

With the action verb **have** we cannot use **got** and we cannot use a short form.

NOT ~~Ming has got lunch around one~~ and NOT ~~I've cereal every morning.~~

The action verb **have** can also be progressive.

Ming **is having** lunch now.   We **were having** a conversation in English.
What time **are** you **having** your party?

In negatives and questions in simple tenses, we use a form of **do**.

We **didn't have** a very good time.   We **don't have** parties very often.
Where **do** you **have** lunch?   How often **does** Liem **have** strange dreams?

In English we often use expressions like **have a talk** instead of a verb like **talk**. Here are some examples.

Shall we **have a drink**?   I usually **have a nap** in the afternoon.
I **had a talk** with Khalid.   Oscar and Angela **are having an argument**.

Practice

A Have and have got (1–2)

Look at the pictures and write positive or negative sentences with *have* or *have got*.
Use these objects: *a car, a map, a rabbit, a ticket, an umbrella*

▶ ..He's got a ticket......... OR ..He has a ticket...........
1 .... 3 ....
2 .... 4 ....

B Have and have got (1–2)

Complete the dialogue. Write the negative or question forms.
Use *have got* for the present and *have* for the past.

Hong: Do you (▶) ..have............ a bike?
Dominic: Yes, but I don't ride it very often.
Hong: (1) .... it .... lights on the front and back?
Dominic: Yes, why?
Hong: Can I leave my bike here and take yours? Mine (2) .... any lights.
          It (3) .... any when I bought it. I meant to get some last week,
          but I (4) .... time.
Dominic: But it's raining now. And you (5) .... a coat. I'll drive you home,
          Hong.

C The verb have (1–3)

Complete the conversation. Use *have/have got* or the action verb *have*.

Zulima: (▶) ..You've got........ (you/have) an empty plate, Sean. Would you like some more food?
Sean: Oh, yes please. I must say, (1) .... (we/have) a great time.
         Luckily (2) .... (you/have) lots of room in here.
Zulima: Yes, it's a nice big apartment, although (3) .... (it/not/have)
         a balcony.
Mark: How was Brazil? (4) .... (you/have) a good vacation?
Zulima: Yes, (5) .... (I/have) a great time, thank you.
Sean: (6) .... (you/have) some photos here to show us?
Zulima: Yes, you should (7) .... (have) a look at them some time. But I was
         so busy having fun (8) .... (I/not/have) time to take very many.

Yes/no questions

1 Use

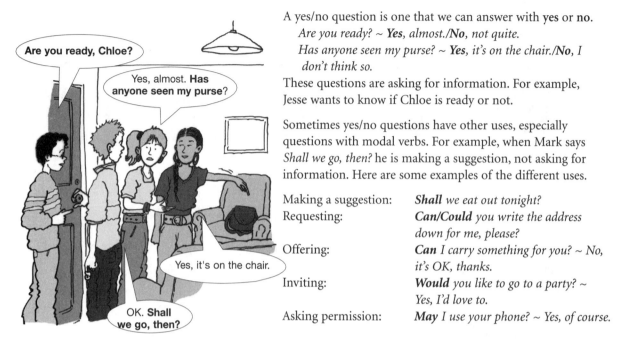

A yes/no question is one that we can answer with **yes** or **no**.
> *Are you ready? ~ **Yes**, almost./**No**, not quite.*
> *Has anyone seen my purse? ~ **Yes**, it's on the chair./**No**, I don't think so.*

These questions are asking for information. For example, Jesse wants to know if Chloe is ready or not.

Sometimes yes/no questions have other uses, especially questions with modal verbs. For example, when Mark says *Shall we go, then?* he is making a suggestion, not asking for information. Here are some examples of the different uses.

Making a suggestion:	***Shall*** *we eat out tonight?*
Requesting:	***Can/Could*** *you write the address down for me, please?*
Offering:	***Can*** *I carry something for you? ~ No, it's OK, thanks.*
Inviting:	***Would*** *you like to go to a party? ~ Yes, I'd love to.*
Asking permission:	***May*** *I use your phone? ~ Yes, of course.*

2 Form

A yes/no question begins with an auxiliary verb. An auxiliary verb is a form of **be** or **have** or a modal verb, e.g. **can**. The auxiliary verb comes before the subject.

AUXILIARY	SUBJECT	VERB		
Is	*it*	*raining?*	STATEMENT:	*It* [*is*] *raining.*
Has	*Baljit*	*bought a car?*		
Can	*Julia*	*drive?*	QUESTION:	[*Is*] *it raining?*

The main verb **be** also comes before the subject in a question.
> ***Is*** *it cold out there?* ***Are*** *you ready?* ***Was*** *it easy?*

If there is more than one auxiliary verb, only the first one comes before the subject.
> ***Have*** *you been working?* ***Could*** *we have done better?*

In the Simple Present and Simple Past we use a form of **do**.

AUXILIARY	SUBJECT	VERB		
Do	*the buses*	*run every day?*	STATEMENT:	*They* [*(do)*] *run every day.*
Does	*Phil*	*play golf?*		
Did	*you*	*like the concert?*	QUESTION:	[*Do*] *they run every day?*

A question cannot begin with an ordinary verb such as **run**, **play**, or **like**.
> NOT *Plays Phil golf?* and NOT *Liked you the concert?*

The verb after the subject does not end in **-s** or **-ed**.
> NOT *Does Phil plays golf?* and NOT *Did you liked the concert?*

Practice

A Use (1)

Write down the use of each question. Choose from these uses:
asking for information (x3), asking permission, inviting, making a suggestion, offering, requesting (x2)

► Could you pick up my dry cleaning? *requesting*
► Can we get a number 35 bus from this stop? *asking for information*
1 Can I help you with those bags? ....
2 Shall we stop for a rest? ....
3 Is it Tuesday today? ....
4 Could you wait a moment, please? ....
5 Would you like to have coffee with us? ....
6 Will your friend be here next weekend? ....
7 May I sit down? ....

B Form (2)

Claude Pheneuf, the World Quiz Champion, is going to be on Guy's talk show.
Guy is wondering what to ask Claude. Read what Guy is thinking and write down his questions.

► (I assume Claude has won lots of prizes.) *Have you won lots of prizes?*
1 (I wonder if he's a rich man.) ....
2 (Perhaps quiz shows are his only hobby.) ....
3 (I believe he worked hard in school.) ....
4 (I wonder if he's got any other interests.) ....
5 (I wonder if it's an interesting life.) ....
6 (Perhaps his wife asks him quiz questions.) ....
7 (And maybe he answers questions in his dreams.) ....

C Yes/no questions (1–2)

What would you say in these situations?

► You want to know if Mark has been to New Brunswick. Ask Sarah.
   Has Mark been to New Brunswick?
1 You aren't sure if Rachel and Vicky are going to Mexico. Ask them.
   ....
2 You want to know if Laura plays tennis. Ask Justin.
   ....
3 You are wondering if Isaac enjoyed his vacation. Ask him.
   ....
4 You want to suggest to Leticia that you both go for a walk.
   ....
5 You need to know if Royson will be at the club tonight. Ask him.
   ....
6 You want to know if the train is on time. Ask Alain.
   ....
7 You are wondering if Sam and Kathryn go camping. Ask Joe.
   ....
8 You want to ask Sotiris if you can borrow his squash racquet.
   ....
9 You want to know if Nick has a motorcycle. Ask him.
   ....

Short answers

1 Answering **yes** or **no**

Look at the answers to these questions.

> *Is it snowing?* ~ **Yes.**   *Are we going to be late?* ~ **Yes, we are.**
>
> *Did you say something?* ~ **No.**   *Did you finish the crossword?* ~ **No, I didn't.**

We can sometimes answer a question with a simple **yes** or **no**, but we often use a short answer like **No, I didn't**. We usually put a comma after **yes** or **no**.

We do not normally use a full sentence, but we can if we want to add emphasis to the answer.

> *Did you open my letter?* ~ **No, I didn't open your letter.**

Sometimes, to be polite, we may need to add information.

> *Did you get the tickets?* ~ No, I didn't. **There wasn't time, I'm afraid. Sorry.**

2 Form

A positive short answer is **yes** + a pronoun + an auxiliary.

QUESTION		SHORT ANSWER		
Auxiliary			Pronoun	Auxiliary
Are	you working tomorrow?	~ Yes,	I	am.
Has	Jen been to Paris?	~ Yes,	she	has.
Will	I need my passport?	~ Yes,	you	will.
Did	they fix your phone?	~ Yes,	they	did.

We can also use the main verb **be** in a short answer.

> **Is** *it time to go?* ~ **Yes, it is.** *It's eleven-fifteen.*

Note that in the Simple Present and Simple Past we use a form of **do**.

> **Do** *you like classical music?* ~ Yes, I **do**. NOT *Yes, I like.*

A negative short answer is **no** + a pronoun + an auxiliary + **n't**.

QUESTION		SHORT ANSWER		
Auxiliary			Pronoun	Auxiliary + n't
Is	the photocopier working now?	~ No,	it	isn't.
Have	the children gone to sleep?	~ No,	they	haven't.
Will	there be food at the party?	~ No,	there	won't.
Does	this train stop at Surrey?	~ No,	it	doesn't.

But note: **No, I'm not.**

> *Are you working tomorrow?* ~ **No, I'm not.** NOT *No, I amn't.*

3 Answering requests, suggestions, offers, and invitations

To answer a request, suggestion, etc., we normally use a phrase like **Yes, of course** or **Yes, please** rather than a short answer. If we answer in the negative, we have to give some explanation.

Request: *Could you help me move these chairs, please?* ~ Yes, of course. OR *I'm afraid I'm busy.*
Suggestion: *Shall we have some coffee?* ~ Yes, OK. OR *Sorry, I can't. I have to go.*
Offer: *Can I give you a hand?* ~ Yes, please. That's very thoughtful. OR *It's OK, thanks. I can manage.*
Invitation: *Would you like to come to the barbecue?* ~ Yes, please. I'd love to. OR *I'd love to, but I'll be away.*

Short negative answers would sound strange or impolite here.

Practice

A Form (2)

It's eleven o'clock, and everyone has arrived at a party. Write the short answers.

▶ Do you have a drink? ~ ...*Yes, I do*......., thank you. I've just put it down somewhere.
1 Can you speak Arabic? ~ ...., but not very well.
2 Is it snowing outside? ~ .... It's just started.
3 Did Andre come with you? ~ .... He's in the hospital, actually.
4 Did you come by car, Tomas? ~ .... It took forever because of all the traffic.
5 Are those people over there your friends? ~ .... I don't know them at all.
6 Do you like Canada? ~ .... I'm enjoying my stay here.
7 Is your brother here? ~ .... He's away on business right now.
8 Have you seen Nick recently? ~ .... I think he's moved away.

B Form (2)

It's one o'clock in the morning, and the party is in full swing. People are still talking. Write the short answers.

▶ Are you French? ~ *No, I'm not*...... I'm Italian. I'm from Milan.
1 Will you and Neil be here in August? ~ .... We're going to Quebec.
2 Did you remember to bring the photos? ~ .... I'll give them to you in a minute.
3 Has Rita broken up with her boyfriend? ~ .... It's all over, she told me.
4 Did you see that documentary about the arctic on television last night?
   ~ .... I was working late, unfortunately.
5 Does Pinder like these old songs? ~ .... She loves the Guess Who.
6 Are you and Mike staying the night here? ~ .... We have to get home tonight.
7 Can we afford a taxi? ~ .... It's a long drive.
8 Are you OK, Audrey? ~ .... I feel really awful.

C Answering questions (1–3)

Which would normally be the best answer?

▶ Are you busy today?
   a) ☐ Yes, busy.   b) ✓ Yes, I am.
1 Is it too hot in here for you?
   a) ☐ No, it isn't.   b) ☐ No, I'm fine, thanks.
2 Do you know Brianna?
   a) ☐ Yes.   b) ☐ Yes, we live in the same building.
3 Tell me, did you steal my money?
   a) ☐ No.   b) ☐ No, I didn't steal your money.
4 Do you live on campus?
   a) ☐ Yes, I do.   b) ☐ Yes, I live on it.
5 Would you like to come out with us for the day?
   a) ☐ Yes, I would like.   b) ☐ Yes, please.
6 Is it the eighteenth today?
   a) ☐ Yes, it is.   b) ☐ Yes, it is the eighteenth of November today.
7 Did you bring my jacket?
   a) ☐ No.   b) ☐ No, sorry. I forgot it.
8 Can I carry your bags?
   a) ☐ No, you can't.   b) ☐ It's all right, thanks.

Question tags

1 Use

Becky: *It's a great day, **isn't it?***
Holly: *Beautiful. We're having a fantastic summer, **aren't we?***
Becky: *You haven't heard a forecast for the weekend, **have you?***
Holly: *No, I haven't, but I think it's going to stay sunny.*

A question tag is a short question added on to a statement. When a tag is spoken, the voice can go down or up.

FALLING	RISING
It's a lovely day, isn't it? ↘	*You haven't heard a forecast, have you?* ↗
With a falling intonation, the speaker thinks the statement is true. Becky knows that it is a lovely day, and she is inviting Holly to continue the conversation. The tag is not really a question.	With a rising intonation, the speaker is less sure. Becky doesn't know if Holly has heard a weather forecast or not. The tag is more like a real question.

2 Form

POSITIVE STATEMENT + NEGATIVE TAG	NEGATIVE STATEMENT + POSITIVE TAG
*It **is** very warm, **isn't** it?*	*It **isn't** very warm, **is** it?*
A negative tag is an auxiliary verb + **n't** + pronoun.	A positive tag is an auxiliary verb + pronoun.
*You've played before, **haven't you?***	*Adeel doesn't have a car, **does he?***
*The children can swim, **can't they?***	*I shouldn't laugh, **should I?***
*It'll be dark soon, **won't it?***	*You aren't sick, **are you?***
*There was a mistake, **wasn't there?***	*The answer wasn't right, **was it?***

The pronoun (**you**, **he**, etc.) refers to the subject of the sentence, e.g. **you**, **Adeel**.

In the Simple Present and Simple Past we use a form of **do**.

*You live near here, **don't you?***	*We don't have to pay, **do we?***
*This coat looks good, **doesn't it?***	*The shower doesn't work, **does it?***
*I turned right, **didn't I?***	*Your horse didn't win, **did it?***

The answer **yes** means that the positive is true, and **no** means that the negative is true.

*Victor works for Zedco, doesn't he? ~ **Yes**, he does. (He **works** for Zedco.)*
*Mythili doesn't eat meat, does she? ~ **Yes**, I think she does. (She **eats** meat.)*
*Kylie is married, isn't she? ~ **No**, of course she isn't. (She **isn't** married.)*
*Matt doesn't have many friends, does he? ~ **No**. (He **doesn't** have many friends.)*

3 Requests and suggestions

After a request with an imperative (e.g. **Wait** …), we can use **would you?** or **could you?**
  Wait** here a minute, **would you?** **Give** me an example, **could you?
We can also use You couldn't …, could you? or You don't …, do you? for a request.
  You couldn't** help me, **could you?** **You don't** have a loonie, **do you?

A Use (1)

Look carefully at each statement and tag. Decide if it is more likely to be a comment (with falling intonation) or a question (with rising intonation).

► This price list is up to date, isn't it? ~ Yes, it is.   a question

1 It was a great show, wasn't it? ~ Fantastic. I really enjoyed it.   ....

2 These sweaters are nice, aren't they? ~ I like this one.   ....

3 We have time for a coffee, don't we? ~ A quick one, maybe.   ....

4 Let me see, the bus leaves at four-ten, doesn't it? ~ Four-twenty.   ....

B Form (2)

You are at a barbecue. Add tags to help start a friendly conversation.

► These sausages are delicious, aren't they? ~ They certainly are.

► You haven't lived here long, have you? ~ No, only three months.

1 It's quite a big yard, ...? ~ Yes, there's lots of room.

2 There aren't many people here yet, ...? ~ No, but it's still quite early.

3 You're Scott's friend, ...? ~ Yes, I'm Bruce.

4 You came in a sports car, ...? ~ That's right.

5 These burgers look good, ...? ~ I can't wait to try them.

6 We can sit on the grass, ...? ~ I think it's dry enough.

7 The weather forecast wasn't very good, ...? ~ No, it wasn't.

C Form (2)

Complete the conversation. Write the question tags.

Chantal: You don't really want to go out with me anymore, (►) ...do you........... ?

Gautam: Of course I do. But I need a bit of time to myself sometimes.

Chantal: You get plenty of time to yourself, (1) ....?

Gautam: Chantal, you know what I feel for you. I've told you enough times,
(2) ....?

Chantal: Yes, you have. And you're happy, (3) ....?
You don't mind, (4) ....? The situation doesn't bother you,
(5) ....?

Gautam: Why are we arguing? There's nothing to argue about, (6) ....?

Chantal: You can't ever look at things from my point of view, (7) ....?

D Requests and suggestions (3)

What would you say in these situations? Write sentences with a question tag. Use the word in parentheses.

► You want to read a newspaper. Daniel might have one, so ask him. (don't)
You don't have a newspaper, do you? ....

1 Suggest to Betty that you both listen to some music. (Let's)
....

2 You need a bus schedule. Marta might have one, so ask her. (don't)
....

3 Ask Leah to pass you the salt. (Pass)
....

So/Neither do I and I think so

1 So and neither

Patricia: *I'm hungry.*
Lily: ***So am I**. I haven't eaten anything all day.*
Paolo: ***Neither have I**. I didn't have time for breakfast.*

We use **so** after a positive statement and **neither** after a negative one.

> *I'm hungry. ~ **So am I**. (= And I'm hungry./I'm hungry, too.)*
> *I **haven't** eaten. ~ **Neither** have I. (= And I haven't eaten./I haven't eaten either.)*

The structure is **so/neither** + an auxiliary + the subject.
The auxiliary is a form of **be** or **have** or a modal verb, e.g. **can**.

> *We're really busy at work. ~ **So are we**.*
> *Jeff has gone to the game. ~ And **so has Craig**.*
> *Dino can't drive, and **neither can Alyssa**.*

The subject comes at the end. NOT *We're busy. ~ ~~So we are.~~*
In the Simple Present and Simple Past we use a form of **do**.

> *I love old cowboy movies. ~ **So do I**.   This phone doesn't work. ~ **Neither does this one**.*
> *I went to the Calgary Stampede, and **so did** Federica.*

We can use **nor** instead of **neither**.

> *Wendy isn't here tonight. **Neither/Nor** is Christopher.*

2 I think so, etc.

Charlotte: *Will we be home in time to watch* The National?
Garrett: ***I think so.** We don't have far to go now.*
Rosa: *We might miss the beginning.*
Charlotte: *Oh, **I hope not**. I haven't watched the news all week.*

Here *I think **so*** means "I think we'll be back in time," and *I hope **not*** means "I hope we don't miss the beginning."

We can use **so** after **be afraid, believe, expect, guess, hope, suppose**, and **think**.

> *Do you think you'll get the job? ~ Well, I **hope so**.*
> *Are you going on vacation this year? ~ Yes, I **believe so**.*
> *I don't know for sure if Geraldine is rich, but I **think so**.*

But we cannot use **so** after **know** or **be sure**.

> *There's been an accident. ~ Yes, **I know**. NOT ~~I know so.~~*
> *Are you sure you're doing the right thing? ~ Yes, **I'm sure**. NOT ~~I'm sure so.~~*

There are two negative structures.

NEGATIVE + **so**	POSITIVE + **not**
*Is it raining? ~ I **don't think so**.*	*Is it raining? ~ I **hope not**.*
*Are you going to the concert? ~ I **don't believe so**.*	*Have we won a prize? ~ I'm **afraid not**.*
With **believe** and **think**, we normally use the negative and **so**.	With **be afraid, guess**, and **hope**, we use the positive and **not**.

We can use **suppose** in either structure.

> *Will there be any seats left? ~ I **don't suppose so**. OR I **suppose not**.*

Practice

A So and neither (1)

Glen has just met Jessica at a party. They are finding out that they have a lot in common.
Write the structures with *so* and *neither*.

    Glen: I haven't been to a party forever.

▶ Jessica: _Neither have I_ . I hate crowded rooms.

▶ Glen: Yes, _so do I_ . I'm not a party-goer, really.

1 Jessica: No, ... I can't make small talk.

2 Glen: .... You know, I'm a very shy person.

3 Jessica: And .... I lead a pretty quiet life.

4 Glen: Well, ... I don't have many friends.

5 Jessica: .... And I would really like a good friend.

6 Glen: Oh, ...

B So and neither (1)

Look at the table and complete the sentences.

	Akeil	Jenny	Emili	Riyaad
Music	✓	✗	✗	✓
Travel	✓	✓	✗	✗
Skiing	✗	✓	✓	✗
Cooking	✗	✗	✓	✓

▶ Jenny can ski, and _so can Emili._

▶ Akeil doesn't like cooking, and _neither does Jenny._

1 Emili doesn't like travelling much, and ....

2 Akeil has lots of CDs, and ....

3 Riyaad can't ski, and ....

4 Jenny isn't a music lover, and ....

5 Emili cooks often, and ....

6 Akeil travels a lot, and ....

C I think so, etc. (2)

Complete these short conversations. Write structures with *so* or *not* and use the words in parentheses.

▶ Lin: Does the library open on Saturdays? (think)

  Saleem: Yes, _I think so_ . But I'm not absolutely sure.

▶ Sabrina: You can't go out for dinner wearing shorts. (guess)

  Naeem: _I guess not_ . I'd better put some pants on.

1 Katie: Will there be a lot of people at the concert tonight? (expect)

  Will: .... There aren't usually very many.

2 Steve: Are you going to apply for the job? (suppose)

  Kathleen: .... It's the only one available.

3 Doug: Do you think it's going to rain? (hope)

  Adrienne: Well, ... I'm just about to go out.

4 Neil: Will the game take place in this weather? (think)

  Vance: .... In fact, I'm sure it won't.

5 Claire: Is my dry cleaning ready, please? (afraid)

  Assistant: .... We're having problems with the machine.

Permission: can, may, could, and be allowed to

1 Asking permission

We use **can**, **could**, or **may** to ask for permission.

> *Can I use your pen?*
> *Could we borrow your ladder, please? ~ Well, I'm using it right now.*
> *May I see the letter? ~ Of course.*

Could often sounds more polite than **can**. **May** is formal.

2 Giving and refusing permission

To give permission we use **can** or **may** (but not **could**).

> *You **can** wait in my office if you like.*
> *Could I borrow your calculator? ~ Of course you **can**.*
> *You **may** telephone from here. (a written notice)*

May is formal and is not often used in speech.

To refuse permission we use **can't** or **may not** (but not **couldn't**).

> *Could we have a picnic here? ~ I'm sorry. I'm afraid you **can't**.*
> *Members **may not** bring more than two guests into the club.*

We can also use **must not**.

> *Luggage **must not** be left unattended.*

You may call
from here

Bicycles must not
be left here

3 Talking about permission

We sometimes talk about rules made by someone else. To do this we use **can**, **could**, and **be allowed to**.

We use **can** to talk about the present, and we use **could** for the past.

Present: *Each passenger **can** take one bag onto the plane.*
Past: *In the 1960s you **could** drive without wearing a seatbelt.*

We can also use **be allowed to**.

Present: *Passengers **are allowed to** take one bag onto the plane.*
Future: ***Will** I **be allowed to** record the interview?*
Past: *We **weren't allowed** to look around the factory yesterday.*

For a general permission in the past we use either **could** or **was/were allowed to**.

> *I **could** always stay/I **was** always **allowed to** stay up late as a child.*

But to say that the permission resulted in a particular action, something that really happened, we use **was/were allowed to** (but not **could**).

> *I **was allowed to** leave work early yesterday.*
> *We **were allowed to** go into the control room when we looked around the power station.*

Compare these questions with **may** and **be allowed to**.

ASKING FOR PERMISSION	ASKING ABOUT PERMISSION
***May** I take a picture of you?* (= Will you allow it?)	*Are we **allowed to** take pictures?* (= What is the rule?)

Practice

A Asking permission (1)

How would you ask for permission in these situations?
Use *Can I ...?*, *Could I ...?*, or *May I ...?* and these verbs: *borrow, join, look at, use*

▶ You are at a friend's house. You want to make a phone call.
  Can I use your phone?

1 You need a calculator. The person sitting next to you has one.

   ....

2 You walk into a restaurant. Three people who you know from work are sitting at a table. You go over to the table.

   ....

3 You had to go to a lecture, but you were sick. Your friend went to the lecture and took notes. The next day you are well again and you see your friend.

   ....

B Giving and refusing permission (2)

A police officer is telling you what the signs mean. What does she say?
Use *can* and *can't* and these verbs: *drop, go, have, park, play, smoke, turn*

Policeman:
▶ You can't go this way. ....
▶ You can park here. ....
1 ....
2 ....
3 ....
4 ....
5 ....

C Be allowed to (3)

Write the correct forms.

James: I hear you've moved into a new apartment with a couple of friends.

Tracey: Yes, it's a nice place, but the landlady is really strict. (▶) *We aren't allowed to do*
(we/not/allow/do) anything. It was my birthday last month, and
(1) .... (I/not/allow/have) a party.

James: Oh, (2) .... (we/allow/have) parties at our place,
luckily. (3) .... (we/allow/do) anything, more or less.
We're hoping to have an all-night party soon, but I'm not absolutely sure if
(4) .... (we/allow/have) it.

D May I ...? or Am I allowed to ...? (3)

Are you asking for permission, or are you asking what the rule is? Write *May I ...?* or
Am I allowed to ...?

▶ *May I* .... use your computer?
▶ *Am I allowed to* .... eat in the office?
1 .... cross the road here?
2 .... ask you a personal question?
3 .... rollerblade in this park?
4 .... drive a car without insurance?
5 .... read your magazine?

Necessity: have to and must

1 Present, past, and future

We use **must** and **have to/has to** to say that something is necessary.

*We're very busy at the office. I **have to** work on Saturday morning.*
*Will **has to** get the car fixed. There's something wrong with the brakes.*
*You'll be graduating soon. You **must** think about your future.*

When we use the past, or the future with **will**, we need a form of **have to**.

*Toshi **had to** go to the dentist yesterday.* NOT ~~She must go to the dentist yesterday.~~
*That wasn't very good. We'**ll have to** do better next time.*

And in other structures we also use a form of **have to**, not **must**.

To-infinitive:	*I don't want **to have to** wait in line for ages.*
After a modal verb:	*Emma has a toothache. She **might have to** go to the dentist.*
Present Perfect:	*Mark **has had to** drive all the way to Peace River.*

For negatives and questions with **have to/has to** and **had to**, we use a form of **do**.

*I **don't have to** work on Sundays.*   *Why **does** Karim **have to** study every evening?*
***Did** you **have to** pay for your second cup of coffee? ~ No, I didn't.*

I don't have to work means that it is not necessary for me to work (see page 48).

2 Must or have to?

Both **must** and **have to** express necessity, but we use them differently.

MUST	HAVE TO
We use **must** when the speaker feels that something is necessary.	We use **have to** when the situation makes something necessary.
*You **must** exercise. (I'm telling you.)*	*I **have to** exercise. (The doctor told me.)*
*We **must** be quiet. (I'm telling you.)*	*We **have to** be quiet. (That's the rule.)*
I/we **must** can also express a wish.	
*I **must** buy a newspaper. I want to check my investments.*	*I **have to** buy a newspaper. My boss asked me to get one.*
*We **must** invite Divina. She's a lot of fun.*	*We **have to** invite Melissa and Brian. They invited us last time.*

3 Have got to

Have got to means the same as **have to**, but **have got to** is informal and is less common than **have**. We use it mainly in the present.

*I **have to**/I'**ve got to** make my sandwiches.*   *My father **has to**/**has got to** take these pills.*
***Do** we **have to** apply/**Have** we **got to** apply for a visa?*

Practice

A Have to (1)

Complete the conversations. Use the words in parentheses and a form of *have to*.

▶ Nikola: Jeff has broken his leg. He had to go .... (he/go) to the hospital.

Jack: Oh no! How long will he have to stay ..... (will/he/stay) there?

Nikola: I don't know.

1 Rayissa: I parked my car outside the hairdresser's, and while I was in there, the car got towed. I've got it back now. But .... (I/pay) a lot of money.

Phil: How much .... (you/pay)?

Rayissa: Two hundred dollars!

2 Rob: That door doesn't shut right. .... (you/slam) it every time.

Twilla: .... (you/will/fix) it then, won't you?

3 Jessica: You're always taking financial courses. Why .... (you/take) so many?

Andrew: .... (I/will/take) a lot more if I want a good job.

4 Adeel: We're in a new house now. .... (we/move). The old place was too small.

Sasha: Did it take you long to find a house?

Adeel: No, we found one easily. .... (we/not/look) very hard. But it was in bad condition. .... (we've/do) a lot of work on it.

5 Frank: My brother .... (start) work at five o'clock in the morning.

Karla: That's pretty early. What time .... (he/get) up?

Frank: Three-thirty.

B Must and have to (2)

Write a sentence with *must*, *have to*, or *has to*.

▶ The sign says, "Passengers must show their tickets."
So passengers have to show their tickets. ....

▶ The children have to be in bed by nine.
Their parents said, "You must be in bed by nine." ....

1 Genane has to get to work on time.
Her boss told her, ...

2 The police told Gary, "You must keep your dog under control."
So Gary ....

3 The students have to listen carefully.
The teacher says, ...

4 The new sign says, "Visitors must report to the security officer."
So now ....

C Must or have to? (2)

Write *must* or *have to/has to*. Choose the best option for the situation.

▶ I have to .... go to the airport. I'm meeting someone.

1 You .... lock the door when you go out. There've been a lot of break-ins recently.

2 Albert .... go to the bank. He doesn't have any money.

3 I .... work late tomorrow. We're very busy at the office.

4 You really .... make less noise. I'm trying to concentrate.

5 I think you .... pay to park here. I'll just go and read that sign.

6 You really .... hurry up, Phoebe. We don't want to be late.

7 I .... turn on the heat. I feel really cold.

Necessity: **must not, don't have to, don't need to**

1 Must not

We use **must** to say that something is necessary (see page 46).

> You **must** be careful with those glasses.   I **must** remember my key.

We use **must not** /ˈmʌsnt/ to say that something is a bad idea.

> You **must not** drop those glasses. They'll break.
> I **must not** forget my key, or I won't get in.

2 Don't have to and don't need to

We can use **don't have to** and **don't need to** when something is not necessary.

> You **don't have to/don't need to** wash those glasses. They're clean.
> Anwar **doesn't have to/doesn't need to** finish the report today. He can do it on the weekend.

For the past we use **didn't**.

> The food was free. We **didn't have to** pay/We **didn't need to** pay for it.

Sometimes we can use **didn't need to** when the action happened, even though it was not necessary.

> Josiah **didn't need to** take the train, but he did anyway. He doesn't like to drive all day.

Practice

A Must, must not, or don't need to? (1–2)

Write *must*, *must not*, or *don't need to*.

▶ Laura: You <u>don't need to</u> take an umbrella. It isn't going to rain.
Trevor: Well, I don't know. It might.
Laura: Don't lose it, then. You <u>must not</u> leave it on the bus.

1 Vicky: Come on. We .... hurry. We .... be late.
Rachel: It's only quarter after. We .... hurry. There's lots of time.

2 Claire: My sister and I are going a different way.
Guide: Oh, you .... go off on your own. It isn't safe. We .... keep together in a group.

3 David: I'll put these cups in the dishwasher.
Melanie: No, you .... put them in there. It might damage them. In fact, we .... wash them at all. We didn't use them.

4 Secretary: I .... forget to type this letter.
Mark: Yes, it .... go in the mail today because it's urgent. But the report isn't so important. You .... type the report today.

B Don't have to (2)

An elderly woman is talking to a reporter from her local newspaper. She is comparing life today with life in the past. Complete her sentences using *don't have to*, *doesn't have to*, or *didn't have to*.

▶ We had to entertain ourselves in the old days. There wasn't any television then. These days people <u>don't have to entertain themselves.</u>

1 There's so much traffic now. You have to wait forever to cross the road. In those days you

....

2 I had to work long hours when I was young. But children today have it easy.
They ....

3 My father had to work in a factory when he was twelve. Just imagine! Today a twelve-year-old child ....

4 There's so much crime today, isn't there? People have to lock their doors now. It was better in the old days when people ....

5 We had to wash our clothes by hand. There weren't any washing machines, you know. Nowadays people ....

C Don't have to or don't need to (2)

Emily and Noelle are preparing for exam week at college. Complete the following sentences using *must*, *must not*, *don't have to*, *doesn't have to*, *don't need to*, or *doesn't need to*.

▶ Both students take their exams seriously because they <u>must</u> pass all of their classes to continue their studies.

1 Their instructors told them, "you .... cheat on your exam—if you are caught cheating, you will get a zero."

2 Emily .... study very much for her math exam because she is an excellent math student.

3 Noelle knows that she .... get a good night's sleep before her English exam so she can concentrate.

4 Emily and Noelle are pretty well prepared for their history exam—they .... pay a tutor to help them study. They might study together, but they know that they .... take too many study breaks.

5 If a student is sick on the day of an exam, she .... get a doctor's note for the instructor as soon as possible; however, when a student is sick on a regular class day, she .... bring a doctor's note.

Passive verb forms

1 Introduction

A passive verb is a form of **be** + a past participle, e.g. **is baked**, **was worn**. Some participles are irregular (see pages 125–26).

2 Summary of verb tenses

	ACTIVE	PASSIVE
Simple Present:	We **bake** the bread here.	The bread **is baked** here.
Present Progressive:	We **are baking** the bread.	The bread **is being baked**.
Present Perfect:	We **have baked** the bread.	The bread **has been baked**.
Simple Past:	We **baked** the bread yesterday.	The bread **was baked** yesterday.
Past Progressive:	We **were baking** the bread.	The bread **was being baked**.
Past Perfect:	We **had baked** the bread.	The bread **had been baked**.

We form negatives and questions in the same way as in active sentences.
> The bread **isn't baked** in a factory. The jacket **hasn't been worn** for years.
> Where is the bread **baked**? Has the jacket ever **been worn** by anyone else?

3 The future and modal verbs in the passive

We use **be** + a past participle after **will**, **be going to**, **can**, **must**, **have to**, **should**, etc.
> The doors **will be closed** this evening. This garbage **should be thrown** away.
> The machine **has to be fixed**. The news **might be announced** soon.
> Seats **may not be reserved**. How **can** the problem **be solved**?

	ACTIVE	PASSIVE
Future:	We **will bake** the bread next.	The bread **will be baked** next.
	We **are going to bake** the bread.	The bread **is going to be baked**.
Modal verb:	We **should bake** the bread soon.	The bread **should be baked** soon.
	We **ought to bake** the bread.	The bread **ought to be baked**.

4 The passive with get

We sometimes use **get** in the passive instead of **be**.
> Lots of mail carriers **get bitten** by dogs. I'm always **getting chosen** for the worst jobs.
> Last week Garrick **got moved** to another department.

Get is informal. We often use it for something happening by accident or unexpectedly.

In negatives and questions in the Simple Present and Simple Past, we use a form of **do**.
> The windows **don't get cleaned** very often. How **did** the painting **get damaged**?

We also use **get** in these expressions: **get dressed/changed**, **get engaged/married/divorced**, **get started** (= start), **get lost** (= lose one's way).
> Shannon and Jeff might **get married**. Without a map we soon **got lost**.

Practice

A Present Progressive passive (2)

Look at the pictures and describe what is happening. Use these subjects: *the car*, *dinner*, *a flag*, *some houses*, *the seals*. Use these verbs: *build*, *feed*, *raise*, *fix*, *serve*.

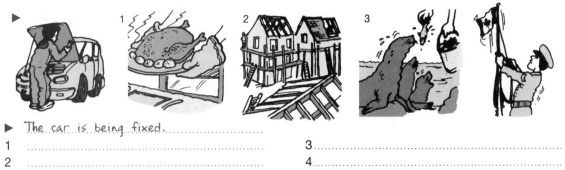

► The car is being fixed.

1 ....   3 ....

2 ....   4 ....

B Passive verb tenses (2)

Complete the information about Casa Loma. Write the correct form of these verbs.

► *build*	2 *use*	4 *not look*	6 *use*
(Simple Past)	(Past Progressive)	(Past Perfect)	(Simple Present)
1 *own*	3 *lease*	5 *do*	
(Simple Present)	(Simple Past)	(Present Perfect)	

The building on the hill near Spadina is Casa Loma, which (►) was built .... in 1911. Today
the house (1) .... by the City of Toronto. It (2) .... by
the Kiwanis Club after it (3) .... by the club in 1937. In the past, the house
(4) .... after very well. Since then, a lot of work (5) ....
on it, and these days the house (6) .... as a popular tourist attraction.

C The future and modal verbs in the passive (3)

A press conference is being held. Write the correct form of the verbs.

► Reporter: Can this new drug prolong human life?

Professor: Yes, we believe that human life can be prolonged .... by the drug.

1 Reporter: Are you going to do any more tests on the drug?

Professor: Yes, further tests .... soon.

2 Reporter: What .... the drug ....?

Professor: It will be called Bio-Meg.

3 Reporter: Can people buy the drug now?

Professor: No, it .... by the public yet.

4 Reporter: Do you think the company should sell this drug?

Professor: Yes, I think Bio-Meg .... to anyone who wants it.

D The passive with get (4)

Write *get* or *got* and the past participle of these verbs: *break*, *change*, *divorce*, *hurt*, *lose*

► If we're going out to the theatre, I'd better get changed ....

1 Jay .... when he tried to break up a fight.

2 I know the way. We won't ....

3 You'd better wrap up the glasses so they don't ....

4 They were only married a year before they ....

Have something done

1 Introduction

Compare these situations.

Svetlana painted the room.
(She did the work herself.)

*Svetlana **had** the room **painted**.*
(A painter did the work.)

We can use **have** in a passive structure. *Svetlana had the room painted* means
that she hired a painter to do it for her as a professional service.

2 Form

Look at these examples.

	HAVE	SOMETHING	DONE	
You should	**have**	your car	**serviced**	regularly.
Marvin usually	**has**	his suits	**cleaned**	at Superclean.
We	**had**	the television	**fixed**	last year.
You've	**had**	your hair	**cut**.	
Our neighbours are	**having**	a new garage	**built**.	
Is Grace	**having**	a new stove	**installed**?	

Note that we can use the perfect or the progressive (**have had, are having**).

In negatives and questions in simple tenses, we use a form of **do**.
> Marvin **doesn't have** his suits cleaned at Fastclean.
> We **didn't have** new windows put in because it was too expensive.
> **Do** you **have** your car serviced regularly?   Where **did** you **have** your hair cut?

3 Get something done

We can also use **get something done**.
> We should **have** another key **made**. OR We should **get** another key **made**.

The sentences have the same meaning, but **get** is more informal than **have**.

Here are some more examples with **get**.
> Lin **got** her shoes **fixed**.   We'**re getting** the carpet **cleaned**.
> Where **did** you **get** your hair **cut**?   Do you **get** your furnace **checked** every year?

4 Have meaning "experience"

We can use **have** in this structure with the meaning "experience something," often something unpleasant.
> We **had** all our money **stolen**.   The car **had** its mirror **knocked** off.

Practice

A Have something done (1–2)

Look at the pictures and describe what people are doing or what they did.
Use these phrases: *her photo*, *his windows*, *his car*, *her eyes*, *his hair*
Use these verbs: *clean*, *cut*, *fix*, *take*, *test*

▶ Right now, Julian *is having his hair cut.* ....

1 Last week Gilbert ....

2 Right now Leslie ....

3 Yesterday David ....

4 Right now Janice ....

B Have something done (1–2)

Read about each situation and write sentences with *have something done*.

▶ Jung-Ha is paying the man who fixed her bicycle.
  Jung-Ha has had her bicycle fixed. ....

1 Diego went to the hospital. A nurse bandaged his arm.

  ....

2 Craig is going to the dentist. She's going to fill his cavity.

  ....

3 Rose is walking around town while her photos are being developed.

  ....

C Get something done (3)

Look again at Exercise B. The jobs are all done now. Complete the questions using *get*.

▶ Miguel: Where *did you get your bicycle fixed, Jung-Ha?* ....

1 Shauna: Why ....

2 Arlynne: Where ....

3 Kathy: Where ....

D Have meaning "experience" (4)

Say what happened to these people.

▶ Corinne (whose luggage was searched in customs)
  Corinne had her luggage searched in customs. ....

1 Jacob (whose car was stolen from outside his house)

  ....

2 Rita (whose rent was increased by ten percent)

  ....

3 David (whose hydro has been cut off)

  ....

Verb + **to**-infinitive

1 Introduction

I've **decided to play** a round of golf. I'm **going to meet** Nadam.

But you **promised to come** shopping this afternoon. I **want to look** for a new sofa.

After some verbs we can use a **to**-infinitive, e.g. **decided to play, going to meet.** Here are some more examples.

> I **expect to get** my money back.
> Genane **agreed to work** late at the office.
> We can't **afford to go** to Australia.
> Are you **hoping to get** a job in Calgary?
> Jen has **offered to help** us when we move.

We can put **not** before the **to**-infinitive.

> Some people just choose **not to get** married.
> At least I managed **not to lose** my temper.

With some other verbs we use an **-ing** form, not a **to**-infinitive (see page 56).

> Steve has **finished playing** golf.

2 **Seem** and **appear**

We can use a **to**-infinitive after **seem** and **appear.**

> Tina **seemed to be** quite annoyed.   The computer program **appears to have** a bug in it.
> The person I spoke to **didn't seem to know** anything about the company's products.

We can use a progressive or a perfect **to**-infinitive.

Progressive: *Jean-Marc seems **to be studying** even harder these days.*
Perfect: *David appeared to **have hurt** himself.*

3 **Tend, manage,** and **fail**

We use **tend to** for things that usually happen.

> We **tend to get** up later on weekends. (= We usually get up later on weekends.)

We use **manage to** for being able to do something.

> Luckily I **managed to find** my way here all right. (= I was able to find my way.)

We use **fail to** for things that don't happen.

> David **failed to pay** his gas bill. (= David didn't pay his gas bill.)

4 He promised to go, his promise to go

Some nouns can come before a **to**-infinitive. Compare these sentences.

Verb + **to**-infinitive: *Steve **promised to go** shopping.*
                            *But then he **decided to play** golf.*
Noun + **to**-infinitive: *Steve forgot about his **promise to go** shopping.*
                            *Sharon found out about his **decision to play** golf.*

Here are some nouns we can use: **agreement, arrangement, decision, demand, desire, failure, offer, plan, promise, refusal, tendency, threat**

Practice

A Verb + to-infinitive (1)

Describe what each speaker did. Use these verbs before a *to*-infinitive: *decide, demand, offer, promise, threaten*

▶ Frank: I must speak to the manager.
   Frank demanded to speak to the manager.

1 Wayne: I'll mow the lawn soon, I promise.

   ....

2 Kathryn: OK, I'll buy both dresses.

   ....

3 Kim: I'll cook dinner, if you'd like.

   ....

4 Ken: If you don't do your homework, Nick, I'll give you an extra assignment.

   ....

B Seem (2)

Complete the answers using *seem* and a *to*-infinitive.
(Some of the *to*-infinitives may be progressive or perfect.)

▶ Vicky: Have Cheryl and Jason apologized to each other?
   Daniel: I think so. They seem to have apologized.
▶ Rita: Is Claire in love with Henry?
   Sarah: Probably not. She doesn't seem to be .... in love with him.
1 Lan: Do Dale and Teri really believe there's life on Mars?
   Ruth: Well, yes. .... there is.
2 Victor: Has Su-Jin's English improved?
   Ethan: Yes, ... a lot.
3 David: Does Rita like basketball?
   Tyrell: I don't think so. .... it much.
4 Natasha: Do you think Lee is working hard?
   Rachel: Yes, I think so. .... hard.
5 Sian: Has Miguel been taking care of his new dog?
   Laura: Not really. .... care of it.

C Verb + to-infinitive (1–4)

Write the *to*-infinitive form. (Some may be progressive or perfect.)
Use these verbs: *come, find, hang, have, invite, leave, take*

Hannah: Hello, Adil. Did you manage (▶) to find .... our apartment easily?
Adil: Yes, in the end. Your directions were a bit confusing, though.
Hannah: Well you're here now. Do you want (1) .... your coat up?
Adil: Thank you.
Hannah: I'm glad you decided (2) .... to our party. Everyone seems
         (3) .... a good time. We tend (4) ....
         lots of people to our parties.
Adil: Is Matt here?
Hannah: No, he couldn't come. He'd already made plans (5) ....
         his brother to the airport.
Adil: And Rita?
Hannah: She was here, but she appears (6) .... early. I don't know
         where she's gone. She was with someone.

Verb + -ing form

1 Introduction

Who **suggested going** camping in October?

I did. But I didn't know it was going to rain. I don't **like putting** up a tent in the rain.

After some verbs we can use an **-ing** form; for example, **suggested going, like putting**.

*I usually **avoid driving** during rush hour.*   *We'll have to **practise throwing** the ball into the basket.*
*Have you **finished typing** that letter?*   *Nick says he's **given up smoking**.*

We can sometimes put **not** before an **-ing** form.

*Imagine **not having** anywhere to live.*

With some other verbs we use a **to**-infinitive, not an **-ing** form (page 54).

*I don't **want to put** up a tent in the rain.*

2 Mind

We use **mind** + an **-ing** form mostly in negative statements and in questions.

*Melissa doesn't **mind having** lots of work. She likes it.*
(= She doesn't dislike having lots of work.)
*Do you **mind waiting** a minute? ~ No, that's OK.*
*I wouldn't **mind travelling** around the world some time.*

3 Verbs with can't

Note **can't** or **couldn't** with **help, resist, face**, and **stand**. We can put an **-ing** form after these verbs.

*I think Jeff is very funny. I **can't help laughing** at his stories.*
*The dress was so beautiful that Mona **couldn't resist buying** it.*
*Let's eat out. I **can't face cooking** dinner today.*
*I never go in the bank if it's busy. I **can't stand waiting** in line.*

4 Keep (on)

We use **keep** or **keep on** + an **-ing** form to talk about something continuing, or when it happens again and again.

*Just **keep stirring** the mixture until it boils.*   *Tommy **keeps calling** Rita and asking her out.*
*The runners didn't mind the rain. They just **kept on running**.*

Practice

A Verb + -ing form (1)

Answer the questions using the notes in parentheses.

► Mike: Is your car working now? (they/not/finish/fix/it)
You: No, they haven't finished fixing it .... yet.

1 Laura: Have you finished the crossword puzzle? (I/give up/try)
You: No, ...

2 Shan: There's a story here in the paper about a 110-year-old man. (I/can/not/imagine/be)
You: Wow. ....so old.

3 Sasha: Do you like hockey? (I/enjoy/watch/it/on TV)
You: Well, ...

4 Rachel: Whose idea was it to invite all these people? (suggest/have/a party)
You: I'm not sure. Someone ....

B Verbs with can't (3)

Use three words from the table to complete each sentence.

1	2	3
can't	face	doing
couldn't	help	feeling
	resist	having
	stand	lying
		noticing

► Raissa said she was OK, but I couldn't help noticing .... how upset she looked.

1 I hate tropical vacations. I .... on a beach all day.

2 I feel really full. I'm afraid I .... a doughnut with my lunch.

3 I was so tired yesterday I just .... any housework.

4 Doug's car was stolen, but since he left it unlocked, I ....
that it's his own fault.

C Verb + -ing form (1–4)

Some friends have had dinner together in a restaurant. Write the -ing forms.
Use these verbs: *change, discuss, eat, get, miss, call, try, wait, walk*

Cindy: Is everyone ready to go?

Alex: Vince hasn't finished (►) eating .... yet.

Vince: It's OK. It's just some mousse.

Adeel: Mousse? After that enormous meal?

Vince: I know. I ate too much. When I find something new on the menu, I just can't resist
(1) .... it.

Alex: How are we getting home?

Cindy: I don't mind (2) .... I feel like some fresh air.

Alex: You're crazy. It's three kilometres. And we've just eaten.

Adeel: I suggest (3) .... for a taxi. It'll save us from (4) ....
around for a bus.

Riyaad: Good idea. I couldn't face (5) .... cold again after being inside all evening.

Alex: Yes, the bus trip is too complicated. It involves (6) .... buses on Victoria
Street. We don't want to risk (7) .... a bus and having to wait half an hour.

Vince: Or we could take a taxi to the bus station and then get a bus from there.

Adeel: Well, you can keep (8) .... the problem, but I'm going to call for a taxi.

Countable and uncountable nouns

1 What is the difference?

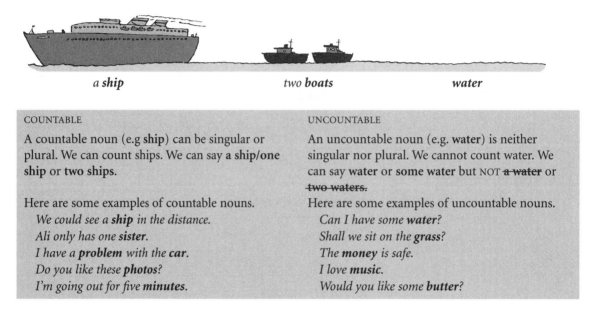

*a **ship***   two **boats**   *water*

COUNTABLE	UNCOUNTABLE
A countable noun (e.g **ship**) can be singular or plural. We can count ships. We can say **a ship/one ship** or **two ships**.	An uncountable noun (e.g. **water**) is neither singular nor plural. We cannot count water. We can say **water** or **some water** but NOT ~~a water~~ or ~~two waters.~~
Here are some examples of countable nouns. *We could see a **ship** in the distance.* *Ali only has one **sister**.* *I have a **problem** with the **car**.* *Do you like these **photos**?* *I'm going out for five **minutes**.*	Here are some examples of uncountable nouns. *Can I have some **water**?* *Shall we sit on the **grass**?* *The **money** is safe.* *I love **music**.* *Would you like some **butter**?*

2 Nouns after **the, a/an**, and numbers

There are some words that go with both countable and uncountable nouns. One of these is **the**.
We can say **the ship** (singular), **the ships** (plural), or **the water** (uncountable). But other words go with one kind of noun but not with the other.

COUNTABLE	UNCOUNTABLE
A/an or **one** goes only with a singular noun. *I need **a spoon**.* Numbers above one go only with plural nouns. *We eat **three meals** a day.*	We do not use **a/an** with an uncountable noun. NOT ~~a water~~ and NOT ~~a music~~. We do not use numbers with an uncountable noun. NOT ~~three foods~~

3 Nouns after **some, many/much**, etc.

Some and **any** go with plural or uncountable nouns. We can also use plural and uncountable nouns on their own, without **some** or **any**.

PLURAL	UNCOUNTABLE
*Ben told **some jokes**.* *Do you know **any jokes**?* *Ben usually tells **jokes**.* But NOT ~~He told joke.~~	*We had **some fun**.* *That won't be **any fun**.* *We always have **fun**.*
Many and **a few** go only with plural nouns. *There weren't **many bottles**.* *I made **a few sandwiches**.*	**Much** and **a little** go with uncountable nouns. *I don't drink **much wine**.* *There was only **a little bread** left.*

Practice

A What is the difference? (1)

Look at the <u>underlined</u> nouns. Are they are countable or uncountable?

► There was a <u>car</u> behind us.   *countable*

► I never eat <u>meat</u>.   *uncountable*

1 Do you play <u>golf</u>?   ....

2 I had to wait ten <u>minutes</u>.   ....

3 Just tell me one <u>thing</u>.   ....

4 <u>Love</u> makes the world go round.   ....

5 Good <u>luck</u> at your new job.   ....

6 Hydro plants produce <u>energy</u>.   ....

7 I'm taking a <u>photo</u>.   ....

8 Would you like an <u>apple</u>?   ....

B A and some (2–3)

Stacy has been to the store. What did she buy? Use *a* or *some* with these words: *banana, cookies, butter, ~~cheese~~, eggs, ~~flowers~~, lemon, light bulb, water, ~~magazine~~, soap, wine*

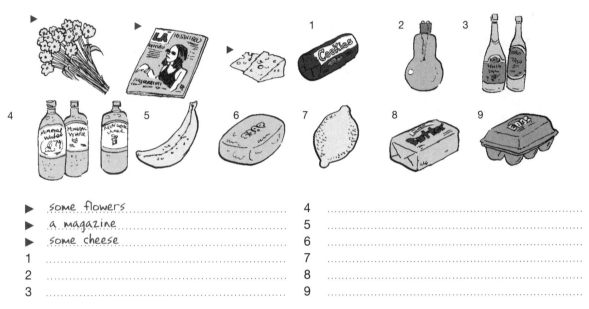

►   some flowers

►   a magazine

►   some cheese

1   ....

2   ....

3   ....

4   ....

5   ....

6   ....

7   ....

8   ....

9   ....

C Countable and uncountable nouns (1–3)

Complete the conversation. Choose the correct form.

Jessica: What are you doing, Saj?

Saj: I'm writing (►) ~~essay~~/an essay.

Jessica: Oh, you've got (1) <u>laptop/a laptop</u>. Do you always write (2) <u>essay/essays</u> on your laptop?

Saj: Yes, but I'm not doing very well today. I've been working on my outline for about three (3) <u>hour/hours</u> now.

Jessica: You've got lots of books to help you, though. I haven't got as (4) <u>many/much</u> books as you do. That's because I don't have much (5) <u>money/moneys</u>. Sometimes I can't even afford to buy (6) <u>food/a food</u>.

Saj: Really? That can't be (7) <u>many/much</u> fun.

Jessica: I'd like to get (8) <u>job/a job</u> I can do in my spare time and earn (9) <u>a/some</u> money. I've got (10) <u>a few/a little</u> ideas, but what do you think I should do?

Saj: I know someone who paints (11) <u>picture/pictures</u> and sells them. Why don't you do that?

Jessica: Because I'm no good at painting.

A carton of milk, a piece of information, etc.

1 A carton of milk

*a **carton of** milk*   *two **cans of** soup*   *a **kilogram of** sugar*   *a **piece/slice of** bread*   *a **loaf of** bread*

Milk, soup, etc. are uncountable nouns. We cannot use **a** or a number in front of them. We do not usually say ~~a milk~~ or ~~two soups~~. But we can say **a carton of milk** or **two cans of soup**. Here are some more examples.

CARTON, TIN, ETC.	MEASUREMENTS	PIECE, SLICE, ETC.
*a **carton of** orange juice*	*a **kilogram of** cheese*	*a **piece of** wood*
*a **can of** paint*	*five **metres of** cable*	*a **piece/slice of** bread*
*a **bottle of** water*	*twenty **litres of** gas*	*a **piece/sheet of** paper*
*a **box of** cereal*	*half a **pound of** butter*	*a **bar of** chocolate*
*a **jar of** jam*		*a **loaf of** bread*
*a **tube of** toothpaste*		
*a **glass of** water*		
*a **cup of** coffee*		

We can also use this structure with a plural noun after **of**.

    *a **bag of** chips*   *a **box of** matches*   *three **kilograms of** potatoes*   *a **collection of** pictures*

2 A piece of information

Advice, information, and **news** are uncountable nouns. We cannot use them with **a/an** or in the plural.

    *Can I give you **some advice**?* NOT ~~an advice~~
    *We got **some information** from the police officer.* NOT ~~some informations~~
    *That's wonderful **news**!* NOT ~~a wonderful news~~

But we can use **piece of, bit of**, and **item of**.

    *Can I give you **a bit of advice**?*
    *There are **two pieces of information** we need to complete the questionnaire.*
    *There's **a bit of/an item of news** that might interest you.*

These nouns are uncountable in English, although they may be countable in other languages:
accommodation, baggage, behaviour, equipment, fun, furniture, garbage, homework, housework, litter, luck, luggage, progress, scenery, traffic, travel, weather, work

Some countable nouns have similar meanings to the uncountable nouns above.

COUNTABLE	UNCOUNTABLE
*There aren't any **jobs**.*	*There isn't any **work**.*
*It's a long **trip**.*	***Travel** can be tiring.*
*There were **sofas** and **chairs** for sale.*	*There was **furniture** for sale.*
*We booked a **room**.*	*We booked some **accommodation**.*
*I've got three **suitcases**.*	*I've got three pieces of **luggage**.*

Practice

A A carton of milk (1)

What did Danny buy at the grocery store? Use *of*.

Milk	2.99
Milk	2.99
1 bag flour	2.20
Jam	3.50
Matches	1.75
Bread	2.12
Bread	2.12
Chocolate	0.95
5 kilograms potatoes	4.29
Breakfast cereal	3.69
Mineral water	1.74
Mineral water	1.74
Toothpaste	1.89
Total	$31.97

▶ *two cartons of milk* ....
▶ *a bag of flour* ....
1 ....
2 ....
3 ....
4 ....
5 ....
6 ....
7 ....
8 ....

B Countable and uncountable nouns (2)

Complete the sentences. Write *a/an* or *some*.

▶ I really ought to do *some*.......... housework.
1 The people who camped here have left .... garbage.
2 I've been working on the business plan. I've made .... progress.
3 The visitors are here for two nights. They're looking for .... accommodation.
4 That store has .... nice sofa.
5 You'll have to pay extra for the taxi because you have .... luggage.
6 The house is empty. I need .... furniture.
7 I can't possibly fit this guitar into .... suitcase.
8 You need .... luck to win the lottery.

C Countable and uncountable nouns (2)

You are talking about the vacation you took with a friend. Use these words:
accommodation, awful trip, beautiful scenery, ~~chair~~, fun, good weather, dinner.
You have to decide whether you need to include *a/an*.

▶ (It was very easy to find a place to stay.)
  Finding ..*accommodation*............. was very easy.
▶ (There was nothing to sit on in your room.)
  But my room wasn't very nice. It didn't even have ..*a chair*.. in it.
1 (You were in a beautiful part of the country.)
  It was a lovely place, though. There was .... all around us.
2 (The weather was good.)
  And we had .... while we were there.
3 (One evening you went to a restaurant with some other people.)
  One evening we had .... with some people we met.
4 (You enjoyed yourselves at the club.)
  We went to a club. We had .... there.
5 (Travelling home was awful.)
  We had .... home last Saturday.

Nouns that can be countable or uncountable

1 A chicken or chicken?

Some nouns can be either countable or uncountable. For example, **a chicken** is a separate, individual thing, but **chicken** cannot be counted.

chicken

a chicken

COUNTABLE	UNCOUNTABLE
*I'm roasting the **chicken**.*	*Would you like **some chicken**?*
*Kajal baked **a cake** for Ken.*	*Have **some cake/a piece of cake**.*
*Adrienne was eating **an apple**.*	*Is there **apple** in this salad?*
*Someone threw **a stone** at the police.*	*The house is built of **stone**.*
*There's **a hair** on your shirt.*	*I must brush my **hair**.* NOT ~~hairs~~

2 A painting or painting?

Often the countable noun is specific, and the uncountable noun is more general.

COUNTABLE	UNCOUNTABLE
*That's **a nice painting** over there.*	*Paul is good at **painting**.*
*We heard **a sudden noise** outside.*	*Constant **noise** can make you sick.*
*Norval Morrisseau had **an interesting life**.*	***Life** is complicated sometimes.*

3 A paper or paper?

Some nouns can be countable or uncountable with different meanings.

COUNTABLE	UNCOUNTABLE
*I bought **a paper**.* (= a newspaper)	*I need **some paper** to write on.*
*I'll have **a glass** of orange juice, please.*	*I bought a piece of **glass** for the window.*
*Do you have **an iron**?* (for clothes)	*The bridge is made of **iron**.*
*I turned all **the lights** on.*	*There's more **light** by the window.*
*I've been to Medicine Hat many **times**.*	*I can't stop. I don't have **time**.*
*The trip was **a great experience**.*	*He has enough **experience** for the job.*
*I run **a small business**.* (= a company)	*I enjoy doing **business**.* (= buying and selling)
*We finally found **a space** in the parking lot.*	*There's no **space** for a piano in here.*
	*There are hundreds of satellites out in **space**.*

4 A coffee or coffee?

Words for drinks are usually uncountable: ***Coffee** is more expensive than **tea**.*
But when we are ordering or offering drinks, we can say either **a cup of coffee** or **a coffee**.

   ***Two coffees**, please.* (= two <u>cups of</u> coffee)   *Would you like **a beer**?* (= <u>a glass/bottle/can of</u> beer)

Some nouns can be countable when we are talking about a particular kind or about different kinds.

   *Chianti is **an Italian wine**.* (= a <u>kind of</u> Italian wine)
   *The use of **plastics** has greatly increased.* (= the use of different <u>kinds of</u> plastic)

Practice

A A chicken or chicken? A painting or painting? (1–2)

Complete the conversations. Choose the correct form.

▶ Can I pick <u>an apple</u>/~~some apple~~ from your tree? ~ Yes, of course.
1 I think <u>coffee/a coffee</u> is too bitter. ~ Me too. I hate it.
2 We ought to buy <u>some apple/some apples</u>. ~ OK, I'll get them.
3 I think <u>painting/a painting</u> is a fascinating hobby. ~ Well, you're certainly very good at it.
4 Did you hear <u>noise/a noise</u> in the middle of the night? ~ No, I don't think so.
5 Is there <u>cheese/a cheese</u> in this soup? ~ Yes, a little.
6 I had <u>conversation/a conversation</u> with Andrea last night. ~ Oh? What about?
7 Shall I put <u>a chicken/some chicken</u> in your sandwiches? ~ Yes, please.
8 Are you a pacifist? ~ Well, I don't believe in <u>war/a war</u>, so I suppose I am.
9 It isn't fair. ~ No, <u>life/a life</u> just isn't fair, I'm afraid.
10 What's the matter? ~ You've got <u>some egg/some eggs</u> on your shirt.

B A paper or paper? (3)

Complete the conversations. Write these nouns: *business* (x2), *experience* (x2),
glass, *iron*, *light*, *paper*, *space*, *time*. Write *a/an* or *some* before each noun.

▶ Jen: Did you manage to park downtown?
   Shea: It took me forever to find .a. space......... . And all I wanted was to buy .some. paper...
              to wrap this present.
1 Heidi: Are you busy tomorrow?
   Donald: I'm meeting someone at the office. We've got .... to discuss.
2 Chris: Do you think I need to take .... with me for my shirts?
   Adelinda: No, I think the hotel will have one.
3 Tanya: I was going to have some juice, but I can't find ....
   Ruby: If you turned .... on, you might be able to see properly.
4 Fone-Ning: I've never met your brother.
   Sean: Oh, he's usually very busy because he runs .... But he's been
              sick recently. The doctor has ordered him to spend .... resting.
5 Krishna: How did your interview go?
   Simona: Well, I didn't get the job. I think they really wanted someone with
              .... in the field, and I don't have any.
              So it was a bit of a waste of time. And the subway coming back was delayed by an hour.
              That's .... I don't want to repeat.

C Countable or uncountable? (1–4)

Complete Adelfina's postcard to her sister. Choose the correct form.

The island is very peaceful. (▶) <u>Life/~~A life~~</u> is good here. Everybody moves at a nice slow pace. People
have (1) <u>time/a time</u> to stop and talk. It's (2) <u>experience/an experience</u> I won't forget for a long time.
There aren't many stores, so I can't spend all my money, although I did buy (3) <u>painting/a painting</u>
yesterday. Now I'm sitting on the beach reading (4) <u>paper/a paper</u>. The hotel breakfast is so enormous
that I don't need to eat lunch. I just took (5) <u>mango/a mango</u> with me to eat later. I've been trying all
the different (6) <u>fruit/fruits</u> grown in this part of the world, and they're all delicious.

Singular or plural?

1 Clothes, etc.

Some nouns have only a plural form (with **s**) and take a plural verb.

The **clothes were** in the dryer. NOT ~~The clothe was~~ ...
The **goods have** been sent to you direct from our factory. NOT ~~The good has~~ ...
My **belongings are** all packed in suitcases.

> PLURAL NOUNS
>
> **arms** (weapons), **belongings** (the things you own), **clothes**, **congratulations**, **contents** (what is inside something), **customs** (bringing things into a country), **earnings** (money you earn), **goods** (products, things for sale), **outskirts** (the outer part of a city/town), **remains** (what is left), **surroundings** (the environment, the things around you), **thanks**, **troops** (soldiers)

Some nouns have both a singular and a plural form with a difference in meaning.

SINGULAR	PLURAL
Our special price is $10 cheaper than normal. That's a **saving** of $10.	My **savings** are in the bank. I'm going to take out all the money and buy a new car.
The storm did a lot of **damage** to buildings.	The newspaper had to pay $2 million in **damages** after printing untrue stories about a politician.
I have a **pain** in my back. It really hurts.	I checked the figures carefully three times. I took great **pains** to get them exactly right.

2 News, etc.

Some nouns have a plural form (with **s**) but take a singular verb.

The **news was** worse than I had expected. NOT ~~The news were~~ ...
Economics is a difficult subject. NOT ~~Economics are~~ ...

> NOUNS TAKING A SINGULAR VERB
>
> The word **news**
> The subjects **economics**, **mathematics**, **physics**, and **statistics**
> The activities **athletics**, **gymnastics**, and **politics**
> The games **billiards** and **darts**
> The illness **measles**

3 Means, etc.

Some nouns ending in **s** have the same singular and plural form.

This means of transportation **saves** energy.
Both means of transportation **save** energy.
This species of insect **is** quite rare.
All **these species** of insect **are** quite rare.

> NOUNS WITH ONE FORM
>
> **crossroads**, **means**, **series** (e.g. *a series of TV shows*), **species** (kind, type)

A Clothes, etc. (1)

Write the nouns and add -s if necessary.

▶ Claire had to take her luggage through .customs............... (custom).

1 Please accept this gift as an expression of our .... (thank).

2 The woman is demanding .... (damage) for her injuries.

3 The .... (pain) was so bad I called the doctor.

4 The old man carried his few .... (belonging) in a plastic bag.

5 If we pay in cash, there is a .... (saving) of ten percent.

6 More .... (good) should be transported by train instead of by truck.

7 The gas explosion caused some .... (damage) to the houses.

8 We're going to spend all our .... (saving) on a new car.

9 The company always takes .... (pain) to protect its image.

B News, etc. (2)

Look at each group of words and decide what they are part of.

Start your answers with these word parts: *eco...*, *geo...*, *his...*, *mat...*, *phy...*

▶ atoms, energy, heat, light   .physics...

1 algebra, numbers, shapes, products   ....

2 dates, nations, past events, wars   ....

3 industry, money, prices, work   ....

4 the climate, the earth, mountains, rivers   ....

C Clothes, news, etc. (1–2)

Choose the correct verb form.

▶ The news is/~~are~~ on at ten o'clock.

1 These clothes is/are in style.

2 Economics is/are Dana's favourite subject.

3 The troops was/were involved in a training exercise.

4 The contents of the briefcase seems/seem to have disappeared.

5 Darts is/are sometimes played in bars.

6 The leftovers was/were thrown in the compost.

D Clothes, news, means, etc. (1–3)

Complete this email Kristina has received from her sister. Choose the correct forms.

(▶) ~~Thank~~/Thanks for your email. Your news (1) was/were interesting. We must talk soon. What about us? Well, we're living on the (2) outskirt/outskirts of town, not far from the company (3) headquarter/headquarters, where Jeremy works. We spent almost all our (4) saving/savings on the house. That wouldn't matter so much if I hadn't crashed the car last week and done some (5) damage/damages to the front of it. More bills! But at least I wasn't hurt. The house is nice, but the neighbourhood (6) isn't/aren't very attractive. We're on a very busy street.

I'm doing the course I told you about. Statistics (7) is/are an easy subject, I find, but economics (8) gives/give me problems!

A/an and the

1 Introduction

Read this story about an American tourist in Canada.

A man from California was spending *a month* in Canada. One day he checked into *a hotel* in Nanaimo, *a nice town* in *the province* of British Columbia. Then he went out to look around *the place*. But *the man* didn't return to *the hotel*. He disappeared, leaving *a suitcase* full of clothes behind. *The police* were called in, but they were unable to find out what had happened to *the missing tourist*. It was *a mystery*. But two weeks later *the man* walked into *the police station* in Nanaimo. He explained that he was very sorry, but while walking around *the town*, he had got lost. He had also forgotten *the name* of *the hotel* he had booked into. So he had decided to continue with his tour of *the country* and had gone to visit *a friend* in Manitoba before returning to pick up *the suitcase* he had left behind.

A/an goes only with a singular noun. With a plural or an uncountable noun we use **some**.	The goes with both singular and plural nouns and with uncountable nouns.
*He left **a suitcase**.* (singular)	*He needed **the suitcase**.* (singular)
*He left **some suitcases**.* (plural)	*He needed **the suitcases**.* (plural)
*He left **some luggage**.* (uncountable)	*He needed **the luggage**.* (uncountable)

2 Use

When the story first mentions something, the noun has **a** or **an**.

> *A **man** booked into **a hotel** in Nanaimo.*

These phrases are new information. We do not know which man or which hotel.

But when the same thing is mentioned again, the noun has **the**.

> *The **man** didn't return to **the hotel**..*

These phrases are old information. Now we know which man and which hotel—the ones already mentioned earlier in the story. We use **the** when it is clear which one we mean.

A/AN	THE
*Would you like to see **a show**?*	*Would you like to see **the show**?*
(I don't say which show.)	(= the show we already mentioned)
*The cyclist was hit by **a car**.*	*Whose is **the car** outside?*
(I don't say which car.)	("Outside" explains which car I mean.)
*In the office **a phone** was ringing.*	*I was in bed when **the phone** rang.*
(The office has lots of phones.)	(= the phone in my house)
*Does Nikhil have **a backyard**?*	*He was at home in **the backyard**.*
(We do not know if there is one.)	(We know he has one.)
*The train stopped at **a station**.*	*Turn left here to get to **the station**.*
(We don't know which station.)	(= the station in this town)
*We took **a taxi**.*	*We went in **the car**.* (= my/our car)
*We could hear **a noise**.*	*We could hear **the noise** of a party.*
*I wrote the number on **an envelope**.*	*I wrote it on **the back** of an envelope.*

3 A man/he and the man/someone

We use **a/an** + noun or **someone/something** when we aren't saying which one.	We use **the** + noun or **he/she/it** when we know which one.
*A **man/Someone** checked into a hotel.*	*The **man/He** didn't return to the hotel.*
*He left **a suitcase/something** behind.*	*The **suitcase/It** contained clothes.*

Practice

A The use of a/an and the (1–3)

Complete this true story. Write a/an or the.

(►) A..... man decided to rob (1) .... bank in the town where he lived. He walked into (2) .... bank and handed (3) .... note to one of (4) .... cashiers. (5) .... cashier read (6) .... note, which told her to give (7) .... man some money. Afraid that he might have (8) .... gun, she did as she was told. (9) .... man then walked out of (10) .... building, leaving (11) .... note behind. However, he had no time to spend (12) .... money because he was arrested (13) .... same day. He had made (14) .... mistake. He had written (15) .... note on (16) .... back of (17) .... envelope. And on (18) .... other side of (19) .... envelope was his name and address. This clue was enough to help (20) .... detectives on the case.

B A man/he and the man/someone (3)

Replace the sentences which contain an <u>underlined</u> word. Use a/an or the with the word in parentheses.

► We didn't have much time for lunch. David made <u>something</u> for us. (omelette)
David made an omelette for us.

1 They ran the race before they held the long jump. Matthew won <u>it</u> easily. (race)

....

2 The driver turned left. Suddenly <u>someone</u> ran onto the road. (child)

....

3 Taya was lying on the sofa. She was watching <u>something</u> on television. (movie)

....

4 I had to take the subway and then a bus. <u>It</u> was half an hour late. (bus)

....

5 A shoplifter tried to steal some clothes. The camera recorded <u>her</u>. (thief)

....

C The use of a/an and the (1–3)

Complete the conversations. Write a/an or the.

► Kathleen: Look outside. The... sky is getting very dark.
  Steve: I hope there isn't going to be ..a.... storm.
1 Dave: I'm going out for .... walk. Have you seen my shoes?
  Nancy: Yes, they're on .... floor in .... kitchen.
2 Shannon: Would you like .... tomato? There's one in .... fridge.
  Jeff: Oh, yes, please. I'll make myself .... grilled cheese sandwich.
3 Niki: If you're going to .... mall, can you get a copy of this key made?
  Shelley: Yes, I'll take it to .... engraving place.
4 Elaine: I have .... problem with my phone bill. Can I see someone about it?
  Receptionist: Yes, go to .... fifth floor. .... elevator is down the hall.
5 George: I didn't know Melanie had .... dog.
  Jerry: It isn't hers. She's just taking it for a walk while .... owner is away.
6 Vena: I've got .... headache. I've had it all day.
  Linda: Why don't you go to .... walk-in clinic? It's open until six.
7 Andrew: Guess what? I found .... $50 bill on the pavement this morning.
  Christine: You really should take it to .... police station, you know.

Place names and the

1 Introduction

Man: *Could you tell me where **the Starlight Theatre** is, please?*
Rachel: *Yes, it's in **Brock Street**. Go this way and take the second left.*

Whether a name has **the** depends on the kind of place it is—for example, a street (*Brock **Street***) or a theatre (***the** Starlight **Theatre***), a lake (***Lake** Erie*), or an ocean (***the** Atlantic **Ocean***).

Most place names do not have **the**.	Some place names have **the**—for example, a name with the word **theatre** or **ocean**.
North America *Saskatchewan* *Halifax* *Brock **Street*** ***Lake** Erie*	***the** Starlight **Theatre*** ***the** Atlantic **Ocean***

Whether we use **the** can also depend on the structure of the name.

We do not use **the** with a possessive ('s).	We often use **the** in structures with **of**, with an adjective, and with plural names.
*at **Matilda's** Restaurant*	With **of**: ***the** Avenue **of** the Americas* With an adjective: ***the** White House* With a plural: ***the** Bahamas*

2 Continents, countries, islands, states, and counties

Most don't use **the**.	Words like **republic** and **kingdom** have **the**.
*travelling through **Africa*** *a vacation in **Mexico*** *on **Baffin Island** to **Vancouver Island*** *from **Red Deer** in **Windsor***	***the** Irish Republic* ***the** United Kingdom (**the** UK)* Plural names also have **the**. ***the** United States (**the** US)* ***the** Virgin Islands*

3 Regions

Regions ending with the name of a continent or country don't use **the**.	Most other regions have **the**.
Central Asia** **South Wales ***Northern Canada***	***the** West* ***the** Middle East* ***the** Balkans* ***the** South* Phrases with **of** have **the**. ***the** South **of** France*

4 Hills and mountains

Most don't use **the**.	Hill ranges and mountain ranges have **the**.
*She climbed (**Mount**) **Logan**.* *down **Magnetic Hill***	*skiing in **the** Alps* *over **the** Rockies*

5 Lakes, oceans, seas, rivers, and canals

Only lakes don't use **the**.	Seas, oceans, rivers, and canals have **the**.
*near **Lake Huron*** *beside **Great Slave Lake***	***the** Mediterranean (**Sea**)* *across **the** Atlantic (**Ocean**)* ***the** St. Lawrence (**River**) **the** Suez Canal*

6 Cities, towns, suburbs, and villages

Most don't use **the**.
Mississauga is a suburb of *Toronto*.
Victoria is south of *Vancouver*.
We live in *Yellowknife*.

Exceptions are ***The Hague*** and ***The Bronx***.
Note also ***the west side*** (***of a town/city***),
the Oakridge neighbourhood.

7 Roads, streets, squares, and parks

Most don't use **the**.
along *Malden Road*
on *Church Street*
near *Times Square*
through *Stanley Park*

Main roads and numbered roads have **the**.
the Bath road (= the road to Bath)
the Trans-Canada Highway   ***the I-75***

8 Bridges

Many don't use **the**.
over *Confederation Bridge*
on *Mission Bridge*

But there are many exceptions.
across ***the Ambassador Bridge***
the Peace Bridge

9 Stations and airports; important buildings

We do not use the with most stations and
airports; with religious, educational, and official
buildings; or with house names.
to *Union Station*
at *Diefenbaker Airport*
near *St. Mary's Church*
Conestoga College   *Parliament Hill*
Campbell House

Exceptions are names with **of** or with a noun
(*science*) or adjective (*white*).
at ***the University of British Columbia***
the Science Museum
past ***the White House***

10 Theatres, hotels, galleries, and centres

A possessive form (**'s**) doesn't use **the**.
Brewster's (*Mountain Lodge*)
at *Petrie's Theatre*

But usually theatres, hotels, etc. have **the**.
at ***the Festival Theatre***
outside ***the Royal York Hotel***
in ***the Vancouver Art Gallery***
the Eaton Centre

11 Stores and restaurants

Most stores and restaurants don't use **the**.
shopping at *Roots*
at *Tim Hortons*

Names with a noun (*body*, *rainforest*) often have **the**.
at ***the Body Shop***
The Rainforest Café
Note also ***the Bay***

Practice

A Place names and the (2–6)

How much do you know about geography? Write these names: *Andes*, *Mexico City*, *Bahamas*, *Italy*, *Lake Michigan*, *River Nile*, *South*, *Nunavut*, *Tasmania*, *Maritime Provinces*, *West Indies*. Decide if you need *the*.

▶ Iqaluit is the capital of .Nunavut....................... .
▶ Nassau is in .the. Bahamas....................... .
1 Chicago lies on the shore of ....
2 Sicily is a part of ....
3 .... are a mountain range in South America.
4 .... are Nova Scotia, PEI, and New Brunswick.
5 .... is an island to the south of Australia.
6 Jamaica is an island in ....
7 .... flows through Egypt.
8 .... is the capital of Mexico.
9 Toulouse is in .... of France.

B Roads, buildings, etc. (5–10)

Complete these sentences from a guide to Toronto. Write the words and decide if you need *the*.

▶ The train to Ottawa leaves from .Union. Station............... (Union Station).
▶ .The. Canon. Theatre............ (Canon Theatre) is on Yonge Street.
1 You can hike along .... (Don River).
2 Grenadier Pond is in .... (High Park).
3 You can get to .... (Billy Bishop Airport) by ferry.
4 There is a concert stage in .... (Yonge-Dundas Square).
5 Walk a little way along .... (Humber Bridge).
6 From there you get a view of .... (Lake Ontario).
7 You can see a play at .... (Royal Alex Theatre).
8 Honest Ed's is in .... (Annex neighbourhood).
9 .... (Gardiner Expressway) runs east-west.
10 .... (Ritz-Carlton) is a very elegant hotel.

C Roads, buildings, etc. (6–11)

Complete the conversation. Write the words and decide if you need *the*.

Sarah: We've just been to (▶) .the. States........... (States)—to (1) ....
         (New York).
Claire: Oh, really? I was there at Christmas. Were you on vacation?
Sarah: Yes, and we really needed a break. It was wonderful. We saw
         (2) .... (Statue of Liberty), and we walked through
         (3) .... (Central Park). We saw all the sights. We spent
         a day in (4) .... (Metropolitan
         Museum of Art). And we walked along (5) .... (Broadway)
         and around (6) .... (Macy's) department store.
Claire: Where did you stay?
Sarah: In a small hotel near (7) .... (Washington Square), not far from
         (8) .... (New York University).
Claire: Last time I was there I stayed at (9) .... (Paramount). It's a
         nice hotel close to (10) .... (Broadway).

D Roads, buildings, etc. (9–10)

A woman is asking Travis for directions. Write the words and decide if you need *the*.

Woman: Excuse me, can you point me in the direction of (▶) .Parliament. Hill...... (Parliament Hill)?

Travis: Yes, go around (1) .... (Museum of Nature) and then follow

(2) .... (Elgin Street) north. If you walk the wrong way, you'll

come to (3) .... (Rideau Canal). So go north, and you'll arrive at

(4) .... (Parliament Buildings). Look behind them and you'll be

able to see (5) .... (Quebec), across the river.

Woman: Thank you very much.

E Roads, buildings, etc. (7–11)

Look at the addresses and write the sentences.

Useful addresses for visitors to Regina	
Greyhound Bus Station, Saskatchewan Drive	Mosiac Stadium, 10th Avenue
Saskatchewan Science Centre, Powerhouse Drive	Conexus Arts Centre, Lakeshore Drive
RCMP Heritage Centre, Dewdney Avenue	University of Regina, Wascana Drive
Mackenzie Art Gallery, Albert Street	Legislative Building, Legislative Drive

▶ The Greyhound Bus Station is .on. Saskatchewan Drive. ....

1 The Saskatchewan Science Centre ....

2 ....

3 ....

4 ....

5 ....

6 ....

7 ....

F Place names and **the** (2–11)

Write the headlines of the articles in this month's edition of *Sunshine*, a travel magazine.

▶ walk/along/Princes Street	A walk along Princes Street
▶ vacation/in/Bahamas	A vacation in the Bahamas
1 day/at/Canada's Wonderland	....
2 train trip/through/Rockies	....
3 tour/of/White House	....
4 beach/on/Riviera	....
5 shopping trip/to/West Edmonton Mall	....
6 small town/in/France	....
7 trip/across/Golden Gate Bridge	....
8 walk/around/Lake Winnipeg	....
9 visit/to/CN Tower	....
10 hike/across/Newfoundland	....
11 tour/of/National Gallery	....
12 boat trip/along/Fraser River	....

This, that, these, and those

1 Introduction

We use **this** and **these** for things near the speaker (***this** printout **here***). This goes with a singular or uncountable noun, e.g. **this report**. These goes with a plural noun, e.g. **these results**.

We use **that** and **those** for things further away (***that** table **there***). That goes with a singular or uncountable noun, e.g. **that furniture**. Those goes with a plural noun, e.g. **those curtains**.

We can leave out the noun if the meaning is clear.

*I'm just having a look at **this**.*   *__That__'s nice, isn't it?*
*Last month's figures were bad, but **these** are worse.*

2 Places and people

When we are in a place or a situation, we use **this** (not **that**) to refer to it.

*There's a fantastic view from **this** office. Just come to the window.*
***This** party isn't much fun, is it? Want to go home?*

We can use **this** to introduce people and **that** to identify people.

*Javier, **this** is my friend Rena.*   *__That__'s Alan over there.*

On the phone we can use **this** to say who we are and **this** or **that** to ask who the other person is.

*Hello? **This** is Chloe speaking. Who's **this/that**, please?*

3 Time

This/these can mean "near in time" and **that/those** "further away in time."

*I'm working as a tour guide **this** summer. I'm pretty busy **these** days.*
*Do you remember **that** summer we all went to Brazil? **Those** were the days.*
*I can't see you on July third. I'm on vacation **that** week.*

To refer back to something that has just happened or was just mentioned, we normally use **that**.

*What was **that** noise? ~ I didn't hear anything.*
*Angie is on a diet. **That**'s why she doesn't want to eat out with us.*
*I lost my key. ~ Well, **that** was a silly thing to do.*

To refer forward to something that is just going to happen or something that we are going to say, we use **this**.

***This** next show should be very interesting.*
*I don't like to say **this**, but I'm not happy with the service here.*

Practice

A This, that, these, and those (1)

Write each of the words (*this*, *that*, *these*, *those*) in the correct place.

	Near	Further away
Singular	this	
Plural		

B This, that, these, and those (1)

Complete the sentences. Use *this*, *that*, *these*, and *those*, and these nouns:
car, *dog*, *flowers*, *package*, *trees*

▶ ....*That car*.... has crashed.

1 Would you like ....?   3 The house is behind ....

2 I must mail ....   4 Whose .... is ....?

C This, that, these, and those (1–3)

Complete the conversations. Use *this*, *that*, *these*, and *those*.

▶ Martin: Are we going out ...*this*.... evening?
    Darlene: I can't. I'll be working late at the office.

1 Justin: I hear you've got a new apartment.
    Marlene: ....'s right. I just moved in.

2 Stanley: What's the matter?
    Toni: It's .... boots. They don't fit properly. They're hurting my feet.

3 Emily: It's so boring here.
    Ricky: I know. Nothing ever happens in .... place.

4 Ava: What happened? You look terrible.
    Marilyn: You won't believe ...., but I've just seen a ghost.

5 Sabrina: What kind of planes are ....?
    Derek: I don't know. They're too far away to see very well.

6 Gord: The big game is three weeks from today.
    Terry: Sorry, I won't be able to play. I'll be away all .... week.

7 Rob: This is Food-Co. Can I help you?
    Brian: Hello. .... is Brian. Can I speak to Fiona, please?

8 Joe: I've had .... bump on my head ever since someone threw a chair at me.
    Rosa: Someone threw a chair at you? .... wasn't a very nice thing to do.

9 Mike: .... seats aren't very comfortable, are they?
    Kerry: No, I don't think I'll want to sit here very long.

My, your, etc. and mine, yours, etc.

1 Introduction

Julio: *Why did you bring **your** work home? We're going out.*
Genevieve: *I'll do it later. Let's go now. Should we take **my** car?*
Julio: *Well, I'd rather not take **mine**. I think there's something wrong with it.*

My, mine, your, etc. express possession and similar meanings. **My car** means the car belonging to me; **your work** means the work you are doing. **My** comes before a noun, e.g. **my car**. We use **mine** on its own.

	MY, YOUR, ETC.	MINE, YOURS, ETC.
First person singular:	*It's **my** car.*	*It's **mine**.*
Second person singular:	*Here's **your** coat.*	*Here's **yours**.*
Third person singular:	*That's **his** room.*	*That's **his**.*
	*It's **her** money.*	*It's **hers**.*
	*The dog's got **its** food.*	
First person plural:	*That's **our** table.*	*That's **ours**.*
Second person plural:	*Are these **your** tickets?*	*Are these **yours**?*
Third person plural:	*It's **their** camera.*	*It's **theirs**.*

2 Its and it's

We use **its** before a noun to express the idea of belonging.
> *The street is around here somewhere, but I've forgotten **its** name.*

It's is a short form of **it is** or **it has**.
> *I think **it's** time to go.* (= it is)   ***It's** been very warm this winter, hasn't it?* (= it has)

3 My, your with parts of the body and clothes

We normally use **my, your**, etc. with parts of the body and with someone's clothes.
> *Victoria shook **her** head sadly.* NOT ~~Victoria shook the head sadly.~~
> *Someone came up behind me and grabbed **my** arm.*
> *You must take off **your** shoes before you enter a mosque.*

But we usually use **the** in the following structure with a prepositional phrase.

	VERB	PERSON	PREPOSITIONAL PHRASE
Someone	*grabbed*	*me*	*by **the** arm.*
The ball	*hit*	*Mike*	*on **the** head.*

4 Own

We use **own** after **my, your**, etc. to say that something belongs to us and to no one else.
> *Wendy has **her own** calculator. She doesn't borrow mine.* NOT ~~an own calculator~~
> *I don't have a roommate. I've got an apartment of **my own**.* NOT ~~of mine own~~

5 A friend of mine

Look at these examples.
> *Pinder is **a friend of mine**.* (= one of my friends) NOT ~~a friend of me~~
> *Julianna came to the party with **a cousin of hers**.* (= one of her cousins)
> *I borrowed **some magazines of yours**.* (= some of your magazines)

Practice

A My, your, etc. and mine, yours, etc. (1)

Complete the conversation. Write the missing words.

Petra: Did you and (▶) ..your........ friends have a nice vacation?

Carmen: Yes, it was wonderful. We had the best vacation of (1) .... lives. It didn't start very well, though. Daniel forgot to bring (2) .... passport.

Petra: Oh, no. So what happened?

Carmen: Well, luckily he doesn't live far from the airport. He called (3) .... parents, and they brought the passport over in (4) .... car, just in time.

Petra: You remembered (5) ...., I hope.

Carmen: Yes, I had (6) ...., even though I'm usually the one who forgets things. Actually Vanessa thought for a minute that she'd lost (7) .... Luckily it was in (8) .... suitcase. Anyway, in the end we had a wonderful time.

B Its and it's (2)

Write the correct form.

▶ Unfortunately, the town has lost .its........... only theatre.

▶ The meeting won't last long. I'll see you when ..it's......... over.

1 You should return the book to .... owner immediately.

2 We'd like to go out for a walk, but .... raining.

3 I'm not buying this tablecloth because .... got a hole in it.

4 The board has decided that MagiCorp needs to improve .... image.

C Parts of the body and clothes (3)

Write *my*, *your*, etc. or *the*.

▶ I was doing jumping jacks when I fell down and hurt .My........... leg.

▶ Matthew served, and the ball hit Warren on the........... knee.

1 A wasp stung me on .... neck. It really hurt.

2 The mother put both .... arms around the child.

3 Aunt Joan kissed Melissa on .... cheek.

4 The fans were all shouting at the top of .... lungs.

5 Don't just stand there with .... hands in .... pockets.

D My own, a friend of mine, etc. (4–5)

Correct the crossed-out sentences.

▶ We're lucky. ~~We've got an own barbecue.~~
   We've got our own barbecue.

1 I met some nice people. ~~Jenny introduced me to a friend of herself.~~

   ....

2 My friends swim every day. ~~They've got their only pool.~~

   ....

3 I enjoy rock-climbing. ~~It's a favourite hobby to me.~~

   ....

4 I hope Matthew will be here. ~~I've got some books from his.~~

   ....

5 I don't want to share. ~~I'd like my very room.~~

   ....

Some and any

1 Basic use

Some and **any** go before a plural or uncountable noun.

> *There were a bowl and **some** cereal on the table, but there wasn't **any** milk.*

We can also use **some** and **any** without a noun.

> *Gilbert wanted **some** milk, but he couldn't find **any**.*

We normally use **some** in positive sentences and **any** in negative sentences or ones with a negative meaning.

POSITIVE	NEGATIVE
*There's **some** milk in the fridge.*	*I don't have **any** milk. (= I have no milk.)*
*I need **some** stamps. ~ There are **some** in the drawer.*	*I don't have **any** stamps. Do you have **any**?*
*I met **some** interesting people last night.*	*I never meet **any** interesting people.*
*We'll have **some** fun in Banff.*	*We won't have **any** fun without you.*

We can also use **any** in a sentence with **if**.

> *If you have **any** problems, you can discuss them with your group leaders.*
> *I can answer **any** questions. (= If there are any questions, ...)*

In questions we can use either **some** or **any**, but **any** is more common.
We don't know whether the answer will be yes or no.

> *Do we have **any** maple syrup?   Will there be **any** food for the guests?   Did you buy **any** clothes?*

We normally use **some** in offers and requests to make them sound more positive.

> *Would you like **some** coffee?   Could you pick up **some** pears for me?*

We can use **some** in questions when we think the answer might be yes.

> *Did you buy **some** clothes? (Perhaps I know that you went out to buy some.)*

2 Someone, anything, etc.

We choose between **someone** and **anyone**, **something** and **anything**, and **somewhere** and **anywhere** in the same way as between **some** and **any**.

***Someone** has spilled water everywhere.*	*Did **anyone** see what happened?*
*Would you like **something** to eat?*	*We don't have **anything** to eat.*
*Let's go out **somewhere**.*	*Is there **anywhere** we can go?*

3 Another use of any

We can use **any** in a positive sentence to mean "it doesn't matter which."

> *I'm free all day. Call me **any** time you want.*
> ***Any** student will be able to tell you where the college library is.*
> *You can buy these maps at **any** gas station. They all have them.*

We say *any gas station* because all gas stations have the maps. It doesn't matter which one you go to.
They are all equally good.

Look at these examples with **anyone**, **anything**, and **anywhere**.

> *It's a very simple puzzle. **Anyone** could solve it. (= It doesn't matter who.)*
> *What should we have for lunch? ~ Oh, **anything**. I don't care.*
> *Where do we have to sit? ~ We can sit **anywhere**. It doesn't matter.*

Practice

A Basic use (1)

Look at the pictures and describe what people have or don't have. Use *some* or *any*.
Use these words: *cats*, *money*, *gas*, *poison*, *sandwiches*

►   They have / They've got some sandwiches.
►   She doesn't have any money.   2   ....
1   3   ....

B Basic use (1)

Harlan Cooper is a radio DJ. Complete what he is saying. Write *some* or *any*.
That was "I Can't Find (►) .Any........... Love" by Arlene Black. Now, I've had (►) .some.......... emails
asking for something by Midnight Moose. One listener says she hasn't heard (1) ....
Midnight Moose songs on this show for months. Well, I'm going to fix that. And this will be our last
song because there isn't (2) .... more time left. We've had (3) .... great songs
tonight, and I'll be here next week to play (4) .... more. Now here's (5) .... music
from Midnight Moose—"I Never Have (6) .... Luck."

C Some, any, someone, anyone, etc. (1–2)

Complete the conversations. Write *some*, *any*, *anyone*, *someone*, *something*, or *anything*.
►   Brodie: We don't have .any............ bread.
      Yvonne: You'd better go to the store, then. We need .some.......... tomatoes, too.
1   Alyssa: Would you like .... waffles?
      Victoria: Oh, no thank you. They were delicious, but I couldn't eat .... else.
2   Patty: There's .... at the door.
      Mike: Are we expecting .... visitors?
3   Sandy: Has .... offered to help you with these skates?
      Dina: No, but I'd be very grateful for .... advice you can give.
4   Anna: I was looking for ...., and now I can't remember what it was.
      Vince: You said you were looking for .... matches.

D Another use of any (3)

Write *any* + noun, *anyone*, or *anything*.
►   The seats aren't reserved. You can have .any seat......... you like.
►   I don't care what we do today. We can do .anything........... you want.
1   If it's your party, you can invite .... you like.
2   All the buses go to the subway. Take .... that comes along here.
3   This carpet is available in lots of colours. You can have .... you want.
4   My father has the television on all the time. He'll watch ....
5   It doesn't matter which day you call. You can call .... you want.

A lot of, lots of, many, much, (a) few, and (a) little

1 Introduction

A lot of, **lots of**, **many**, and **much** mean a large quantity.

*Galen Weston owns a chain of supermarkets. He's made **a lot of** money.*

A few and **a little** mean a small quantity.

*I'd better hurry. My bus leaves in **a few** minutes.*

Many and **a few** go before plural nouns.		**Much** and **a little** go before uncountable nouns.	
***many** places*	***many** problems*	***much** money*	***much** trouble*
***a few** people*	***a few** buildings*	***a little** snow*	***a little** food*

A lot of and **lots of** go before both plural and uncountable nouns.

***a lot of** tourists*	***lots of** games*	***a lot of** sugar*	***lots of** fun*

We use these words without a noun if it is clear what we mean.

*I take photos, but not as **many** as I used to. At one time I took **a lot**.*

Note that we say **a lot** without **of**.

2 A lot of, many, and much

As a general rule, we use **a lot of** and **lots of** in positive statements and **many** and **much** in negatives and questions.

Positive:	*We get **a lot of** storms here.*	*We get **a lot of** snow here.*
Negative:	*We don't get **many** storms here.*	*We don't get **much** snow here.*
Questions:	*Do you get **many** storms here?*	*Do you get **much** snow here?*
	*How **many** eggs do we need?*	*How **much** salt do we add?*

We use **many** or **much** (not **a lot of**) after **too**, **so**, and **as**.

*There are **too many** cars.*   *I've got **so much** work.*   *I don't have **as much** money as you do.*

In formal English, we can sometimes use **many** and **much** in a positive statement.

***Many** students have financial problems.*   *There is **much** enthusiasm for the idea.*

But this is less common in conversation, where we normally use **a lot of** or **lots of**.

In informal English, you may hear **a lot of** in a negative or a question.

*I don't have **many** friends/**a lot of** friends.*   *Do you eat **much** fruit/**a lot of** fruit?*

3 Few and little with and without a

With **a** the meaning is positive.	Without **a** the meaning is negative.
***A few** customers have come into the store. It has been fairly busy.*	***Few** customers have come into the store. It has been quiet.*
*Marta has made **a little** progress and so is feeling upbeat.*	*Marta has made **little** progress and so is not feeling very upbeat.*
A few customers = some customers, a small number of customers	*Few customers* = not many customers
A little progress = some progress, a small amount of progress	*Little progress* = not much progress

Few and **little** (without **a**) can be very formal. In informal speech we can use these structures.

***Not many** customers have come in.*   *Marta **hasn't** made **much** progress.*

***Only a few** customers have come in.*   *Marta has made **only a little** progress.*

Practice

A A lot of, lots of, many, much, a few, and a little (1)

Correct the crossed-out sentences.

▶ Colin was only spending one night away. ~~He quickly put a little things into a suitcase.~~
He quickly put a few things into a suitcase. ....

1 Eleanor is learning to drive. ~~She hasn't had much lessons yet.~~
....

2 I'm making chowder for twenty people. ~~I'll have to make a lot of.~~
....

3 I feel really tired. ~~I don't have many energy.~~
....

4 The mixture looks dry. ~~Maybe you should add a few water.~~
....

5 We're having a big party. ~~We invited a lots of friends.~~
....

B A lot of, many, and much (1–2)

Complete the conversation. Write *a lot of*, *many*, or *much*. More than one answer may be correct.

Logan: There are (▶) ..a lot of.............. athletes taking part in the International Games in
         Edmonton. There's been (1) .... coverage in the papers.

Jana: Our runners haven't won (2) .... medals, have they?

Logan: No, not as (3) .... as last time. But there's plenty of time. There are
         still (4) .... events to come. I'd like to go and see some of the track
         events, but I don't have (5) .... time these days.

Jana: No, not with exams coming up.

Logan: I'm hoping to go on the weekend if I can get a ticket. Apparently there aren't
         (6) .... seats left.

Jana: I've heard the cheapest tickets are $60. I think that's too (7) ....

C A few, few, a little, and little (3)

Write *a few*, *few*, *a little*, or *little*.

▶ I don't think I can lift this box on my own. I need ..a little.......... help.
▶ ..Few................. tourists visited Northern Ireland in the 1980s because of the terrorism there.
1 The mail carrier doesn't come here often. We receive .... letters.
2 The snow was very deep. There seemed .... hope of completing
  our hike.
3 Dwayne isn't finding it easy to shovel the driveway. He's having ....
  trouble.
4 Sioban is exhausted. She's taking .... days' vacation next week.
5 David likes golf, but unfortunately he has .... ability.
6 I can speak .... words of Cantonese, but I'm not fluent.

D Many, few, much, and little (2–3)

Complete this paragraph from a travel guide. Write *many*, *few*, *much*, or *little*.

The main town on the island is very small and does not have (▶) ..many......... important buildings.
The islanders do not have (1) .... money, and they have (2) .... contact with the
outside world. There is not (3) .... chance of the place attracting large numbers of tourists.
The roads are not very good. There are lots of bicycles but not (4) .... cars. And there are
hardly any of the modern facilities that visitors expect. There are (5) .... stores, and there
is (6) .... entertainment.

Personal pronouns

1 The meaning of the pronouns

Flora: *Hello, Han. Have **you** seen Ariana?*

Han: *I don't think so. No, **I** haven't seen **her** today.*

Flora: ***We**'re supposed to be going out at seven-thirty, and **it**'s almost eight now.*

Han: *Maybe **she** just forgot. **You** know Ariana.*

Flora: ***We**'re going out for dinner. Marco and Yvette said **they** might come, too.*
                 *I hope **they** didn't go without **me**.*

I/me means the speaker, and **you** means the person spoken to.
We/us means the speaker and someone else. Here, **we** = Flora and Ariana.
He/him means a male person and **she/her** a female person. Here, **she** = Ariana.
It means a thing, an action, a situation, or an idea. Here, **it** = the time.
They/them is the plural of **he**, **she**, and **it** and means people or things.

2 Subject and object forms

		FIRST PERSON	SECOND PERSON	THIRD PERSON
Singular	SUBJECT	I	you	he/she/it
	OBJECT	me	you	him/her/it
Plural	SUBJECT	we	you	they
	OBJECT	us	you	them

We use the subject form (**I**, etc.) when the pronoun is the subject and there is a verb.
     ***I** don't think so.*   *Maybe **she** just forgot.*
We use the object form (**me**, etc.) when the pronoun is the object of a verb or preposition.
     *I haven't **seen her** today.*   *I hope they didn't go **without me**.*

The pronoun on its own or after **be** usually has the object form.
     *Who spilled coffee all over the table? ~ **Me**./Sorry. It was **me**.*
Compare this answer.
     *Who spilled coffee all over the table? ~ **I** did.*

3 You, one, and they

We can use **you** or **one** to mean "any person" or "people in general," including the speaker.
     ***You** shouldn't believe what **you** read in the newspapers.*
     OR ***One** shouldn't believe what **one** reads in the newspapers.*
     ***You** don't like/**One** doesn't like to have an argument in public.*
You is normal in conversation. **One** is more formal.

We can use **they** for other people in general.
     ***They** say too much sugar is bad for you.*
We can also use it for people in authority.
     ***They**'re going to build a new swimming pool here.*
They is informal and conversational. We use the passive in more formal situations.
     *A new swimming pool **is going to be built** here.*

Practice

A The meaning of the pronouns (1)

Read the conversation between Garrick and Christina. Decide who or what the <u>underlined</u> pronouns refer to.

Garrick: Have (▶) <u>you</u> been in that new store?

Christina: No, not yet.

Garrick: I haven't either, but (▶) <u>it</u> looks interesting. There's a great shirt in the window, and (1) <u>it</u> isn't expensive.

Christina: Laura bought some jeans there. (2) <u>She</u> said (3) <u>they</u> were really cheap.

Garrick: (4) <u>You</u> ought to go there and take a look, then.

Christina: (5) <u>We</u>'d better not go now or we'll be late. (6) <u>I</u> told Oscar and Miranda we'd meet (7) <u>them</u> at five-thirty.

Garrick: Oh, Tom said (8) <u>he</u>'s coming, too.

▶ you = .Christina...............

▶ it = .the..store...............

1 it = ...

2 she = ...

3 they = ...

4 you = ...

5 we = ...

6 I = ...

7 them = ...

8 he = ...

B Subject and object forms (2)

Complete the conversation. Write the pronouns.

Nick: Did (▶) you....... say that you and Hannah wanted some coloured lights for your party?

Patrick: Yes, but (▶) it......'s OK. Shauna's neighbour Jake has some, and (1) ....'s going to lend (2) .... to (3) ....

Nick: Great. Is Kylie coming to the party?

Patrick: We've invited (4) .... of course, but (5) .... isn't sure if (6) .... can come or not. Her parents are flying somewhere on Saturday night, and she might be taking (7) .... to the airport.

Nick: And what about Hannah's friend Emily?

Patrick: I think (8) ....'ll be there. And her brother. (9) .... both came to our last party.

Nick: Do (10) .... mean Jason? I don't like (11) .... very much.

Patrick: Oh, (12) ....'s OK. But (13) .... don't have to talk to (14) ....

C Subject and object forms (2)

Write the pronouns.

▶ There's no need to shout. I can hear ..you........... .

1 You and I work well together. ....'re a good team.

2 We've got a bit of a problem. Could .... help ...., please?

3 This is a good photo, isn't ....? ~ Is Gloria in ....? ~ Yes, that's .... —, look. ....'s next to Marina.

4 Who did this crossword? ~ .... I did .... this morning.

5 Is this Sharida's purse? ~ No, ... didn't bring one. It can't belong to ....

6 ....'m looking for my shoes. Have .... seen ....? ~ Yes, ...'re here.

D You and they (3)

Complete the conversation. Write you or they.

Scott: I'm not going to drive in this weather. It's too icy.

Richard: (▶) .You...... don't want to take any risks. (1) .... can never be too careful.

Scott: I just heard the weather forecast and (2) .... say there's going to be more snow. (3) ....'re better off indoors in weather like this.

Richard: I think (4) .... ought to clear the snow off the roads more quickly.

There and it

1 There + be

Look at these examples.

> *I really need to get some coffee. ~ Well, **there's** a coffee shop down the street.*
> *Could I make myself an omelette? ~ Of course. **There are** some eggs in the fridge.*
> ***There's** an important meeting at work that I have to go to.*

To talk about the existence of something, we use **there + be**. **Be** agrees with the following noun.

> *There **is** a coffee shop.* BUT *There **are** some eggs.*

Here are some more examples.

> ***There's** a bus at ten-thirty.*　　***There'll be** a meal waiting for us.*
> ***Is there** a washroom in the building?*　　***Were there** any bargains at the store?*
> ***There have been** some burglaries recently.*　　***There might have been** an accident.*

We also use **there** with words like **a lot of, many, much, more, enough**, and with numbers.

> *There were **a lot of** problems to discuss.*　　*There's too **much** noise in here.*
> *Will **there** be **enough** chairs?*　　*There are **thirty** days in April.*

2 Uses of it

We use **it** for a thing, an action, a situation, or an idea.

> *You're wearing a new coat. **It's** very nice.* (it = the coat)
> *Hockey is an expensive sport, isn't **it**?*
> *You have to fill in all these stupid forms. **It's** ridiculous.*
> *I find astrology fascinating. I'm really interested in **it**.*

We use **it** to mean "the unknown person."

> *Did someone call? ~ **It** was Jerusha. She just called to say she got home safely.*

We use **it** for the time, the weather, and distance.

> ***It's** six o'clock already.*　　***It's** one kilometre to the lake.*
> ***It** was much warmer yesterday.*　　***It's** three hours from here to Kingston.*

We also use **it** in structures with a **to**-infinitive or a **that**-clause.

> ***It** was nice **to meet your friends**.*
> ***It** would be a good idea **to book a seat in advance**.*
> ***It's** important **to switch off the electricity**.*
> ***It's** too bad **(that) you can't come with us**.*

This is much more common than, for example, *To meet your friends was nice.*

3 There or it?

We often use **there** when we mention something for the first time, like the picture in this example.

> ***There** was a picture on the wall. **It** was an abstract painting.*

We use **it** when we talk about the details. It means *the picture.*

Here are some more examples.

> ***There's** a woman at the door. ~ Oh, **it's** Aunt Camila.*
> ***There** was a dog in the yard. **It** was a big black one.*
> ***There's** a new filing system at work. **It's** very confusing.*

Practice

A There + be (1)

Look at the pictures and describe what you see. Use these words: *a balloon*, *some boxes*, *the car*, ~~a dinosaur~~, *an elephant*, ~~some flowers~~, *the garden*, ~~her hat~~, *the sky*, ~~the water~~

▶ There's a dinosaur in the water.
▶ There are some flowers on her hat. ..... 2 ....
1 .... 3 ....

B There + be (1)

Write *there* and a form of *be*, e.g. *is*, *are*, *was*, *have been*, or *will be*.

▶ Cesar: Are there .... any restaurants here that stay open late?
  Helena: There's .... a café on Broadview that is open until three in the morning.
1 Ringo: .... a train at twelve-thirty, isn't there? Let's catch that one.
  John: OK. .... time to finish our conversation on the train.
2 Nicole: What happened? Why .... so many police cars here?
  Adrian: .... a robbery at the bank.
3 Chris: Last night .... a party next door. I couldn't get to sleep.
  Heather: .... must .... a lot of people there.

C Uses of it (2)

Rewrite the sentences in parentheses using *it*.

▶ We sometimes go surfing. (Surfing is really fun.) It's really fun. ....
1 I bought a shirt at the mall. (The shirt was very cheap.) ....
2 Someone called. (The caller was Jasmine.) ....
3 Our hot water is shut off. (The situation is very inconvenient.) ....
4 I left my coat at home. (The weather is very warm.) ....
5 Don't lose your credit card. (To keep it somewhere safe is important.)
  ....

D There or it? (3)

Write *there* or *it*.

▶ Is it .... the fifteenth today? ~ No, the sixteenth.
1 The road is closed. ....'s been an accident.
2 Take a taxi. ....'s a long way to the doctor's office.
3 .... was a convertible outside. .... looked very expensive.
4 Will .... be any delays because of the strike? ~ Well, ... would be a good idea
  to call the airline and check.
5 .... was wet, and .... was a cold northerly wind. .... was after
  midnight, and .... were few people on the streets.

The pronoun **one/ones**

1 Introduction

Jay: *Here's that bottle of water you wanted.*
Karen: *Oh, no, this is a small **one**. I wanted a big **one**.*
Jay: *They didn't have any big **ones** at the corner store.*
Karen: *That store never has what I want. Why didn't you go to
         the **one** on Robson Street?*

Here *a small **one*** means "a small bottle," *big **ones*** means "big bottles,"
and *the **one** on Robson Street* means "the store on Robson Street."
We use **one** for a singular noun and **ones** for a plural noun.
We use **one** and **ones** to avoid repeating a noun.

We cannot use **one** or **ones** with an uncountable noun, e.g. **water**.
   *There was no hot water. I had to shower in **cold**.*

2 Structures with **one/ones**

Sometimes we can either use **one/ones** or leave it out.
   *I don't like those paintings. What about **this** (**one**)?*
We can do this after **this**, **that**, **these**, and **those**; after **each** or **another**; after **which**; or
after a superlative, e.g. **easiest**.
   *I don't like these sweaters. I prefer **those** (**ones**) over there.*
   *I tried all three numbers, and **each** (**one**) was busy.*
   *The product is available in all these colours. **Which** (**one**) would you like?*
   *The last question is the **most difficult** (**one**).*

Sometimes we cannot leave out **one/ones**.
   *Our house is the **one** on the left.* NOT ~~Our house is the on the left.~~
We cannot leave out **one/ones** after **the** or **every** or after an adjective.
   *The movie wasn't as good as **the one** we saw last week.*
   *I called all the numbers, and **every one** was busy.*
   *I'd like a box of tissues. A **small one**, please.*
   *I donated my old running shoes and bought some **new ones**.*

3 A small one and one

We can say **a small one**, **a red one**, etc. but NOT ~~a one~~.
   *I've been looking for a toque, but I can't find **a nice one**.*
   *I've been looking for a toque, but I can't find **one**.*
Here we use **one** instead of **a toque**. Here are some more examples.
   *We decided to take a taxi. Luckily there was **one** waiting.*
   *If you want a ticket, I can get **one** for you.*

Now look at these examples with **one**, **some**, **it**, and **them**.
   *I don't have a passport, but I'll need **one**.*   (**one** = a passport)
   *I don't have any stamps, but I'll need **some**.*   (**some** = **some** stamps)
   *I've got my passport. They sent **it** last week.*   (**it** = the passport)
   *I've got the stamps. I put **them** in the drawer.*   (**them** = the stamps)
One and **some/any** are like **a**, but **it** and **they/them** are like **the**. We use **one** and **some/any** when we aren't
saying which, and we use **it** and **they/them** to be specific (when we know which).

Practice

A One (1)

Look at the pictures and complete the conversations.

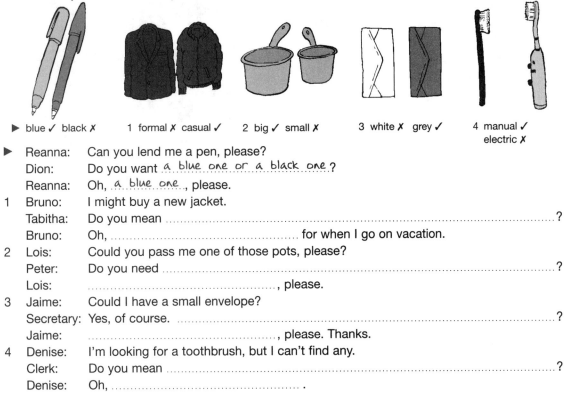

▶ blue ✓ black ✗   1 formal ✗ casual ✓   2 big ✓ small ✗   3 white ✗ grey ✓   4 manual ✓
                                                                                    electric ✗

▶ Reanna: Can you lend me a pen, please?
  Dion: Do you want a blue one or a black one ?
  Reanna: Oh, a blue one , please.
1 Bruno: I might buy a new jacket.
  Tabitha: Do you mean ....?
  Bruno: Oh, ... for when I go on vacation.
2 Lois: Could you pass me one of those pots, please?
  Peter: Do you need ....?
  Lois: ...., please.
3 Jaime: Could I have a small envelope?
  Secretary: Yes, of course. ....?
  Jaime: ...., please. Thanks.
4 Denise: I'm looking for a toothbrush, but I can't find any.
  Clerk: Do you mean ....?
  Denise: Oh, ...

B One and ones (1–3)

Rewrite the sentences in parentheses so that the noun is not repeated. Use *one* or *ones*.
▶ These cups are pretty. Each one is hand-painted. (Each cup is hand-painted.)
1 I need to fill in an application form, but ....(I don't have a form.)
2 I've watched all these movies. ....(I need to get some new movies.)
3 These photos are good. ....(Have you seen this photo?)
4 I need a tuxedo for the party, so ....(I've rented a tuxedo.)
5 Those socks are ugly. ....(Can't you find any nice socks?)
6 This map isn't very good. ....(The map in the car is better.)

C One, some, it, and them (3)

Write *one*, *some*, *it*, or *them*.
▶ I don't know if I'll need any money. I'd better take some ., I suppose.
1 If you need an umbrella, I can lend you ....
2 The radio isn't working. Tamara dropped .... on the floor.
3 I'm buying a beaver tail. Would you like ...., too?
4 I had the matches a minute ago, and now I can't find ....
5 I don't have any blank DVDs, but Jacinta has ....

Adjectives

1 Introduction

*Jeff and Shannon are having dinner in a **quiet** restaurant. It's a **warm** evening. The food is **delicious**. Jeff is feeling **romantic**.*

An adjective is a word like **quiet**, **warm**, **delicious**, **romantic**. The word **quiet** describes the restaurant. It tells us what the restaurant is like.

2 Word order

There are two places where we can use an adjective:
before a noun (*a quiet restaurant*) and after a linking verb (*feeling romantic*).

BEFORE A NOUN	AFTER A LINKING VERB
*Ellissa has a **new car**.*	*Ellissa's car **is new**.*
*It was a **dark night**.*	*It was **getting dark**.*
*This is **good coffee**.*	*This coffee **tastes good**.*
	Some linking verbs are: ***appear**, **be**, **become**, **feel**, **get**, **look**, **seem**, **smell**, **stay**, **taste***

We can use two or more adjectives together (see page 88).
    *It's a **quiet little** restaurant.   Milos was wearing a **dirty old** coat.*

We can put a word like **very** or **quite** before an adjective.
    *It was a **very dark** night.   Jeff was feeling **extremely romantic**.*
Very and **extremely** are adverbs of degree (see page 94).

3 Adjectives used in one position only

We can use most adjectives in both positions—before a noun or after a linking verb. A few adjectives can go in one position but not in the other.

Here are some examples of adjectives which can only go before a noun.
    *Be careful crossing the **main** road.   The **only** problem is that I have no money.*
    *This is an **indoor** game.   The **former** goalie now trains young players.*

Some more examples are: **chief** (= main), **elder** (= older), **eldest** (= oldest), **inner**, **outdoor**, **outer**, **principal** (= main), **upper**

Here are some examples of adjectives which can only go after a linking verb.
    *At last the baby is **asleep**.   Julie's two brothers are very **alike**.*
    *I'm really **pleased** to see you.*

Some more examples are: **afraid**, **alone**, **ashamed**, **awake**, **alive**, **content** (= happy), **fine** (= in good health), **glad**, **unwell**, **well**

Practice

A Adjectives (1)

Look at the pictures and write a phrase with an adjective and noun.
Use these nouns: *building*, *car*, *cat*, *chairs*, *music*, *power*, *skirt*, ~~*weather*~~

▶ long/short	▶ hot/cold	1 traditional/modern	2 black/white
3 hydroelectric/solar	4 classical/pop	5 new/old	6 tall/low

▶ a long skirt ....   3 ....
▶ cold weather ....   4 ....
1 ....   5 ....
2 ....   6 ....

B Adjectives (1–2)

<u>Underline</u> all the adjectives in this description of a hotel.

This ▶ <u>comfortable</u> hotel with its beautiful courtyard is ideal for people who want a quiet vacation,
yet it is only a short distance from the highly popular attractions of the area. There are scenic views
from every room. The atmosphere is very friendly, and the staff are always helpful. A vacation here is
very good value for your money. You can eat your meals at the hotel, where the food tastes amazing.
Or you can of course try some of the excellent local restaurants.

C Adjectives used in one position only (3)

Look at the notes and write the song titles. Sometimes the adjective comes before the noun,
and sometimes you need to use *is* or *are*.

▶ your sister / elder   *Your Elder Sister* ....
▶ this boy / alone   *This Boy is Alone* ....
1 the world / asleep   ....
2 my desire / chief   ....
3 my heart / content   ....
4 the thing to remember / main ....
5 the night / alive   ....
6 secrets / inner   ....
7 the girl for me / only   ....

Adjective order

1 Introduction

It's **beautiful sunny** weather.

Xavier has a **big black** dog.

We can use more than one adjective before a noun. There is usually one correct order. We cannot say ~~sunny beautiful weather~~ or ~~a black big dog~~.

2 Adjectives and nouns

We sometimes use two nouns together.

    a **glass** door   a **computer** program

Here we use **glass** like an adjective, to describe the door. When we use another adjective as well (e.g. **heavy**), it comes before both the nouns.

    a **heavy** glass door   a **useful** computer program

3 Word order

We order adjectives according to their meaning. This is the normal order:

	GROUP	EXAMPLES	
1	Opinion (how good?)	*wonderful, nice, great, awful, terrible*	Adjectives that say how good
2	Size (how big?)	*large, small, long, short, tall*	and how big come first.
3	Most other qualities	*quiet, famous, important, soft, wet, difficult, fast, angry, warm*	Most adjectives come next if they do not belong to another group.
4	Age (how old?)	*new, old*	
5	Colour	*red, blue, green, black*	
6	Origin (where from?)	*Canadian, American, French*	
7	Material (made of?)	*stone, plastic, steel, paper*	Some of these are nouns.
8	Type (what kind?)	an *electric* blanket, *political* party, *road* transportation	
9	Purpose (what for?)	a *bread* knife, a *bath* towel	

Here are some examples.

    a **small green** insect (size, colour)   **Japanese industrial** designers (origin, type)
    a **wonderful new face** cream (opinion, age, purpose)   **useless plastic** souvenirs (opinion, material)
    a **long boring train** ride (size, quality, type)   some **nice easy test** questions (opinion, quality, purpose)
    a **beautiful wooden picture** frame (opinion, material, purpose)

We sometimes put commas between adjectives in Groups 1–3

    a **horrible, ugly** building   a **busy, lively, exciting** city

Practice

A Adjective order (1–3)

Describe the pictures. Use these words: *boots, building, car, bench, singer*

▶ They're leather.
They're big.

1 It's small.
It's white.

2 It's old.
It's attractive.

3 It's wooden.
It's for the garden.
It's expensive.

4 He sings in
the opera.
He's Italian.
He's famous.

1   2   3   4

▶   big leather boots ....
1   3   ....
2   4   ....

B Adjective order (1–3)

Write a list of things to be sold at an auction.

▶   bowl / sugar, antique, silver   an antique silver sugar bowl ....
1   vase / glass, old, lovely   ....
2   mirror / wall, attractive   ....
3   desk / modern, office   ....
4   chairs / kitchen, red, metal   ....
5   boat / model, interesting, old   ....
6   stamps / postage, valuable, Australian   ....
7   table / small, coffee, wooden   ....

C Adjective order (1–3)

Read each ad and write the information in a single sentence.

▶   This game is new. It's for the family. And it's exciting.
     This is an exciting new family game. ....
1   This computer is for an office. It's Japanese. And it's powerful.
     ....
2   This fireplace is electric. It's energy-efficient. And it's small.
     ....
3   This is a chocolate bar. It's new. And it's a big bar.
     ....
4   This show is Canadian. It's on television. And it's terrific.
     ....
5   These doors are aluminum. They're for your garage. And they're stylish.
     ....
6   These shoes are new. They're for sports. And they're wonderful.
     ....
7   This cellphone is small. It's Korean. And it's very good.
     ....

Comparative and superlative forms

1 The comparison of adjectives

We form the comparative and superlative of short adjectives (e.g. **cheap**) and long adjectives (e.g. **expensive**) in different ways.

	COMPARATIVE	SUPERLATIVE
Short word, e.g. *cheap*:	*cheaper*	*(the) cheapest*
Long word, e.g. *expensive*:	*more expensive*	*(the) most expensive*

2 Short and long adjectives

One-syllable adjectives (e.g. **small**, **nice**) usually have the -**er**, -**est** endings.
> *Your cellphone is **smaller**.*   *Monique needs a **bigger** desk.*
> *This is the **nicest** colour.*   *This room is the **warmest**.*

But we use **more**, **most** before words ending in -**ed**.
> *Everyone was pleased with the results, but Phoebe was the **most pleased**.*

We also use **more**, **most** with three-syllable adjectives (e.g. **ex·cit·ing**) and with longer ones.
> *The movie was **more exciting** than the book.*   *This dress is **more elegant**.*
> *We did the **most interesting** project.*   *This machine is the **most reliable**.*

Some two-syllable adjectives have -**er**, -**est**, and some have **more**, **most**. Look at this information.

TWO-SYLLABLE ADJECTIVES

1   Words ending in a consonant + -**y** take -**er**, -**est**, e.g. *happy* → *happ**ier**, happ**iest***
    Examples are: *busy, dirty, easy, funny, happy, heavy, lovely, lucky, pretty, silly, tidy*
2   Some words take -**er**, -**est** OR *more, most*, e.g. *narrow* → *narrow**er**, narrow**est*** OR ***more** narrow,*
    ***most** narrow*
    Examples are: *clever, common, cruel, gentle, narrow, polite, quiet, simple, stupid, tired*
3   The following words take *more, most*, e.g. *useful* → ***more** useful, **most** useful*
    a   Words ending in -**ful** or -**less**, e.g. **careful**, **helpful**, **useful**; **hopeless**
    b   Words ending in -**ing** or -**ed**, e.g. *boring, willing; annoyed, surprised*
    c   Many others, e.g. *afraid, certain, correct, eager, exact, famous, foolish, frequent, modern,*
        nervous, recent

3 Spelling

There are some special spelling rules for the -er and -est endings.

> 1 -e → -er, -est, e.g. *nice* → *nicer, nicest, large* → larg**er**, larg**est**
> Also *brave, fine, safe*, etc.
> 2 -y → -ier, -iest after a consonant, e.g. *happy* → *happier, happiest*
> Also *lovely, lucky, pretty*, etc.
> 3 Words ending in a single vowel letter + single consonant letter → double the consonant
> e.g. *hot* → *hotter, hottest, big* → *bigger, biggest*
> Also *fit, sad, thin, wet*, etc. (but *w* does not change, e.g. *new* → *newer*)

For more details, see page 119.

4 The comparison of adverbs

Some adverbs have the same form as an adjective, e.g. **early, fast, hard, high, late, long, near**.
They form the comparative and superlative with **-er, -est**.
> *Can't you run **faster** than that?*   *Andre works the **hardest**.*

Note also the spelling of **earlier** and **earliest**.

Many adverbs are an adjective + -ly, e.g. **carefully, easily, nicely, slowly**.
They form the comparative and superlative with **more, most**.
> *We could do this **more easily** with a computer.*
> *Of all the players, it was François who planned his strategy the **most carefully**.*

In informal English we use **cheaper, cheapest, louder, loudest, quicker, quickest**, and **slower, slowest** rather than **more cheaply, the most loudly**, etc.
> *Margaret reacted the **quickest**.*   *You should drive **slower** in a blizzard.*

Note the forms **sooner, soonest**, and **more often, most often**.
> *Try to get home **sooner**.*   *I should exercise **more often**.*

5 Irregular forms

Good, well, bad, badly, and **far** have irregular forms.

ADJECTIVE/ADVERB	COMPARATIVE	SUPERLATIVE
good/well	*better*	*best*
bad/badly	*worse*	*worst*
far	*farther/further*	*farthest/furthest*

> *You've got the **best** handwriting.*   *How much **further** are we going?*

We can use **elder, eldest** + noun instead of **older, oldest**, but only for people in the same family.
> *My **elder/older** sister got married last year.*

6 Comparing quantities

We use **more, most** and their opposites **less, least** and **fewer, fewest** to compare quantities.
> *I don't have many books. You've got **more** than I have.*   *The Edgewater Hotel has the **most** rooms.*
> *Ramy spends **less** on clothes than Larissa does.*   *Emma made the **fewest** mistakes.*

Practice

A The comparison of adjectives (1–2)

Complete the sentences. Use these adjectives: *beautiful*, *expensive*, *high*, *interesting*, ~~tall~~

▶ The giraffe is taller than the man.
▶ The computer is more expensive than the book.
1 Detective stories .... than homework.
2 The top of the mountain .... than the clouds.
3 The acrobat .... than the clown.

B The comparison of adjectives (1–2)

Jeff is a Maple Leafs fan. He never stops talking about them. Write the superlative form of each adjective.

▶ Everyone's heard of the Leafs. They're the most famous (famous) team in the NHL.
▶ They've got a long history. They're one of the oldest (old) teams in the league.
1 They bring in lots of money. They're the .... (valuable) NHL team.
2 Their goalie is fantastic. He's the .... (good) goalie in the league.
3 The Leafs are great. They're the .... (great) team ever.
4 And what a team! It's the .... (exciting) team ever.
5 They've got lots of fans. They're the .... (popular) team in the country.
6 The Leafs have won the cup more than 10 times. They're one of the ....
   (successful) teams ever.
7 They're fun to watch. They play the .... (exciting) games.
8 Leafs fans are loyal. We're the .... (loyal) people in the world.

C The comparison of adjectives (1–3)

Complete each ad with the comparative form of the adjective.

▶ Use Get-It-Clean and you'll get your floors cleaner.
▶ Elegant Wallpapers simply look more elegant.
1 Watch a Happy Video and you'll feel ....
2 Wear a pair of Fast Shoes and you'll be a .... runner.
3 Helpful Cookbooks are a .... guide to cooking.
4 Wash your hair with Shiny Shampoo for .... hair.
5 Try a Big-Big Burger and you'll have a .... meal.
6 Restful Beds give you a .... night.
7 Wear Modern Fashions for a .... look.

D The comparison of adverbs (4)

Write the comparative form of these adverbs: *carefully*, *early*, ~~easily~~, ~~high~~, *long*, *loud*, *often*, *well*

▶ I was too nervous to go ..higher. than halfway up the tower.

▶ We could have found the place .more..easily. with a map.

1 Do you have to wear those old jeans, Mike? Can't you dress ....?

2 You needn't go yet. You can stay a bit ....

3 There are lots of break-ins. They happen .... nowadays.

4 If you do it ...., you won't make so many mistakes.

5 The movie starts at eight, but we should get to the theatre a few minutes ....

6 We can't hear. Could you speak a bit ....?

E Irregular forms (5)

Philippe and Agnes are walking in the country. Write *further*, *furthest*, *better*, *best*, *worse*, and *worst*.

Agnes: I'm not used to long walks. How much (▶) ..further. is it?

Philippe: Not far. And it gets better. We've done the (1) .... part. Look, the path
           gets easier. It goes downhill from here. I hope you're feeling (2) ....
           now, Agnes.

Agnes: I feel awful, actually— (3) .... than before.

Philippe: Oh, no. Do you want to take a break?

Agnes: No, the (4) .... thing would be to get home as soon as we can. I'm
           not in very good shape, you know. This is the (5) .... I've walked for
           a long time.

F Comparing quantities (6)

Write *more*, *most*, *less* (x2), and *least*.

Kendra: Our new car is smaller, so it uses (▶) .less. gas. They tested some small cars, and this one
         costs the (1) .... to run of all the cars in the test. It's very economical,
         so Franco likes it. He wants to spend (2) .... money on driving.

Willow: Can you fit three people in the back?

Kendra: Not very easily. We had (3) .... room in our old car.
         (4) .... cars can fit five people, but not this one.

G Comparative and superlative forms (1–6)

Write the correct forms.

▶ You're the ~~luckyest~~ person I know.   luckiest

▶ The situation is getting ~~difficulter~~.   more difficult

1 I was ~~happyer~~ in my old job.   ....

2 I've got the ~~most small~~ office.   ....

3 This photo is the ~~goodest~~.   ....

4 Last week's meeting was ~~more short~~.   ....

5 Money is the ~~importantest~~ thing.   ....

6 Is Bernadette ~~elder~~ than Marina?   ....

7 This game is ~~excitinger~~ than the last one.   ....

8 Of all the students, Elian does the ~~more~~ work.   ....

9 This month has been ~~weter~~ than last month.   ....

10 The prices are ~~more low~~ here.   ....

11 I feel more ~~bad than~~ I did yesterday.   ....

Adverbs of degree

1 Very, pretty, a bit, etc.

*Marisol is a **bit** tired. She's been working all morning.*

*Matteo is **pretty** tired. He's been working all day.*

*Chandra is **very** tired. She had to work late at the office.*

An adverb of degree makes the meaning weaker or stronger. Here are some more examples.

SMALL DEGREE (weaker)	MEDIUM DEGREE	LARGE DEGREE (stronger)
a little late	**fairly** unusual	**absolutely** sure **really** sick
slightly complicated	**pretty** good	**completely** annoyed
	somewhat loud	**extremely** cold

2 Very cold, fairly quickly, etc.

An adverb of degree (e.g. **very**) goes before an adjective (e.g. **cold**) or an adverb (e.g. **quickly**).

ADVERB + ADJECTIVE	ADVERB + ADVERB
*It's **very cold** today.*	*The time passed **very quickly**.*
*Satchi looked **pretty upset**.*	*We go on vacation **fairly soon**.*
*This dress is **absolutely gorgeous**.*	*Our team played **extremely well**.*

Before a comparative we can use **a bit**, **a little**, **a lot**, **far**, **much**, and **slightly**.
> *I'm feeling **a lot better** today.*   *These new trains go **much faster**.*

3 Really hurting, slowly walking, etc.

Some adverbs of degree can describe a verb.
They usually go in mid position.
> *My foot is **really hurting**.*   *Laureen is **slowly walking** to town.*   *I **quite like** this cake.*

Some adverbs of degree go at the end of a sentence when they describe a verb.
They are **a bit**, **a little**, **a lot**, and **much**.
> *Mark **travels a lot**.*   *I'll **open** the window **a little**.*

Absolutely, **completely**, and **totally** can go in mid position or at the end.
> *We **completely** lost our way./We lost our way **completely**.*
> *I **totally** disagree./I disagree **totally**.*

4 Much

Now look at these sentences.
Positive: *I like this town **very much**.* NOT *~~I like this town much.~~*
Negative: *I don't like this town **very much**.* OR *I don't like this town **much**.*
In a positive statement we use **very much**. In a negative statement we can use either **very much** or **much**.

Practice

A Very, pretty, a bit, etc. (1)

Write sentences using one of the phrases in parentheses.

▶   (somewhat hungry or very hungry?) He's somewhat hungry.

1   (a bit busy or very busy?) ....

2   (a bit thirsty or really thirsty?) ....

3   (pretty strong or very strong?) ....

4   (fairly happy or extremely happy?) ....

B Very, pretty, and a bit (1)

Write *very*, *pretty*, or *a bit*.

▶   The bus service is OK. The buses are ...pretty..... frequent.

1   I couldn't sleep because of the awful noise. The club was .... noisy.

2   The weather was OK—at least it didn't rain. It was .... good.

3   The train was almost on time. It was just .... late.

4   Someone paid a lot of money for the house. It was .... expensive.

5   There were some very small traces of mud on the boots. They were .... dirty.

6   There was a medium amount of traffic on the road. It was .... busy.

C Very cold, really hurting, etc. (2–4)

Put the adverbs in the right place. Sometimes more than one answer is correct.

▶   These books are old (very).   These books are very old.

▶   I hate travelling by air (really).   I really hate travelling by air.

1   That radio is loud (a bit).   ....

2   I love my new job (absolutely).   ....

3   Why don't you slow down (a little)?   ....

4   The rain spoiled our day (completely).   ....

5   We did the job quickly (fairly).   ....

6   I feel better now (a lot).   ....

7   We enjoyed the concert (very much).   ....

8   My arms ached (a lot).   ....

D Adverbs of degree (1–4)

Complete the ad for vacation apartments by choosing the correct words.

Why not take this opportunity to buy a wonderful Interlux Timeshare apartment in St. Petersburg? These are (▶) a bit/fairly/really luxurious apartments set in this (1) absolutely/slightly magnificent town, a (2) fairly/really beautiful and sunny place, which you'll like (3) much/very/very much. The apartments are an (4) extremely/pretty/somewhat good value. And we are a company with a (5) fairly/pretty/very good reputation. This is a (6) bit/slightly/totally safe way of investing your money. But hurry! People are buying up the apartments (7) a lot/very/very much quickly.

In, on, and at (place)

1 Meanings

*Mei-Lin is **in** the elevator.*

*Jasper's dog is **on** the rug.*

*There's someone **at** the door.*

IN	ON	AT
in the elevator **in** the kitchen work **in** the garden swim **in** the pool	sit **on** the floor walk **on** the sidewalk a number **on** the door egg **on** your shirt	sit **at** my desk wait **at** the bus stop **at** the intersection wait **at** the traffic lights
In a town/country *Maurice lives **in** St. John's.* *Managua is **in** Nicaragua.* *Does the plane stop **in** Denver?*	On a street **on** King Street On a road or river *a farm **on** this road* *Quebec City is **on** the St. Lawrence.* On a floor (1st, 2nd, etc.) **on** the first floor	At a house/an address **at** Mike's (house) **at** 65 Rumsey Road At a street/landmark on a trip *Does this bus stop **at** the Bourassa Hotel?* At an event **at** the party

2 In and at with buildings

IN	AT
*There are 4000 seats **in** the arena.* *It was raining, so we waited **in** the bar.* We use **in** when we mean inside a building.	*I was **at** the arena.* (= watching a game) *We were **at** the bar.* (= having a drink) But we normally use **at** when we are talking about what happens there.

3 Some common phrases

IN	ON	AT
in prison/the hospital **in** the lesson **in** a book/newspaper **in** the photo/picture **in** the country **in** the middle **in** the back/front of a car **in** a line/row	**on** the platform **on** the farm **on** the page/map **on** the screen **on** the island drive **on** the right/left **on** the back of an envelope **on** a team	**at** the station/airport **at** home/work/school **at** the beach **at** the top/bottom of a hill **at** the back of the room **at** the end of the hall

A Meanings (1)

Look at the pictures and write the sentences. Use *in*, *on*, or *at* and these words:
the bath, *the club*, *the intersection*, *the roof*, ~~*the table*~~

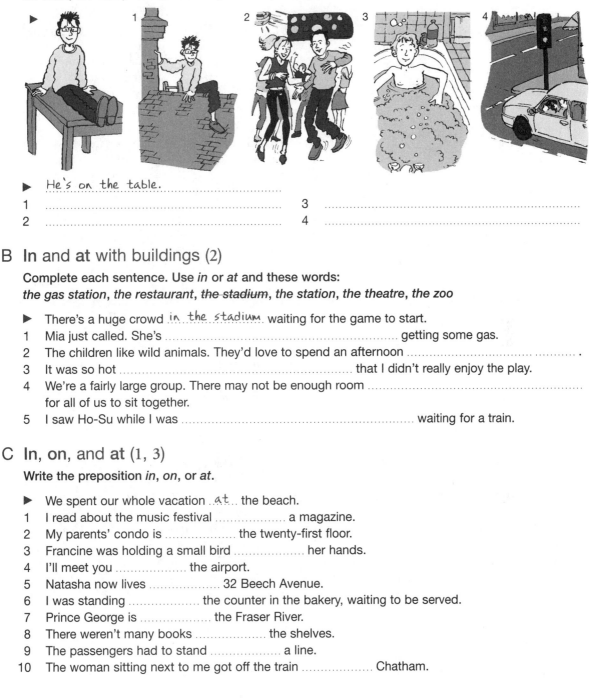

▶ _He's on the table._

1 ....   3 ....
2 ....   4 ....

B In and at with buildings (2)

Complete each sentence. Use *in* or *at* and these words:
the gas station, *the restaurant*, ~~*the stadium*~~, *the station*, *the theatre*, *the zoo*

▶ There's a huge crowd _in the stadium_ waiting for the game to start.
1 Mia just called. She's .... getting some gas.
2 The children like wild animals. They'd love to spend an afternoon ....
3 It was so hot .... that I didn't really enjoy the play.
4 We're a fairly large group. There may not be enough room ....
   for all of us to sit together.
5 I saw Ho-Su while I was .... waiting for a train.

C In, on, and at (1, 3)

Write the preposition *in*, *on*, or *at*.

▶ We spent our whole vacation _at_ the beach.
1 I read about the music festival .... a magazine.
2 My parents' condo is .... the twenty-first floor.
3 Francine was holding a small bird .... her hands.
4 I'll meet you .... the airport.
5 Natasha now lives .... 32 Beech Avenue.
6 I was standing .... the counter in the bakery, waiting to be served.
7 Prince George is .... the Fraser River.
8 There weren't many books .... the shelves.
9 The passengers had to stand .... a line.
10 The woman sitting next to me got off the train .... Chatham.

In, on, and at (time)

1 Saying when

Look at these examples.

IN	ON	AT
*We bought the house **in** 2008.*	*The race is **on** Saturday.*	*The movie starts **at** seven-thirty.*
In + year/month/season	**On** + day/date	**At** + clock time/meal time
in 1988	*on Wednesday*	*at three o'clock*
in September	*on April 15th*	*at breakfast (-time)*
in winter	*on that day*	*at that time*
in the 21st century		*at the moment*
In + a week or more	**On** + a single day/weekend	**At** + two or three days
in the first semester	*on Victoria Day*	*at Easter/Christmas*
in the past week	*on the weekend*	*(= the few days surrounding*
		the holidays)
In + part of day	**On** + day + part of day	
in the morning	*on Friday morning*	
in the evening	*on Tuesday evening*	
Look at these examples with **night**.		
*I woke up **in** the night.*	*It happened **on** Monday night.*	*I can't sleep **at** night.*
(= in the middle of the night)		*(= when it is night)*

But we do not use **in**, **on**, or **at** before **every**, **last**, **next**, **this**, **tomorrow**, and **yesterday**.

*We go to Greece **every summer**.   My brother came home **last summer**.*
*I'll see you **next Friday**.   I finish school **this year**.*
*The party is **tomorrow evening**.   The group left **yesterday morning**.*

2 In time or on time?

IN TIME	ON TIME
In time means "early enough."	**On time** means "at the right time" or "on schedule."
*We'll have to hurry if we want to get there **in time** for the show.*	*The plane took off **on time**.*
	*I hope the meeting starts **on time**.*
*We got to the airport **in time** to have a coffee before checking in.*	*Joni is never **on time**. She's always late.*
*I was about to close the door but I remembered my key just **in time**. (= at the last moment)*	

3 Other uses of in

We can use **in** for the time it takes to complete something.

*I did the crossword **in** five minutes.   Could you walk thirty kilometres **in** a day?*

We can also use **in** for a future time measured from the present.

*Your photos will be ready **in** an hour. (= an hour from now)*
*The building will open **in** six weeks.*

Practice

A Saying when (1)

Read the information about Pierre Laporte and then answer the questions.
Begin each answer with *in*, *on*, or *at*.

Pierre Laporte was born in Montreal. His date of birth was February 25, 1921. The year 1970 saw him become the Deputy Premier of Quebec. That same year, he was kidnapped and killed. The date of his killing was October 17. He was buried in Montreal several days later.

▶ When was Pierre Laporte born? _On February 25, 1921._

1 When did he become Deputy Premier of Quebec? ....
2 When was he killed? ....
3 When was he buried (month)? ....

B Saying when (1)

Giorgio is planning a business meeting. Decide if you need *in*, *on*, or *at*.
If you do not need a preposition, put an (*X*).

Giorgio: I'm sorry I was out when you called (▶) _X_ yesterday afternoon, Alice. Look, I'm free (▶) _on_ March fifteenth. Can we meet then?

Alice: I'm pretty busy (1) .... next week, I'm afraid. I can't see you (2) .... Friday.

Giorgio: I'd like to have a meeting (3) .... this month, if possible. I'll be very busy (4) .... April.

Alice: I'm going away (5) .... Easter, so how about the week after? Shall we meet (6) .... the twenty-seventh? That's a Wednesday.

Giorgio: I've got an appointment (7) .... the morning but nothing (8) .... the afternoon. Let's meet (9) .... Wednesday afternoon (10) .... two-thirty.

C In time or on time? (2)

Write the correct phrase: *in time* or *on time*.

▶ If the plane is late, we won't get to Atlanta _in time_ for our connecting flight.

1 We were up very early, ... to see the sun rise.
2 How can the buses possibly run .... with all these traffic jams?
3 The mail gets picked up at five. I'm hoping to get this letter written ....
4 The train will be here at quarter after twelve if it's ....

D In, on, or at? (1–3)

Complete the conversations using *in*, *on*, or *at*.

▶ Guy: You just bought that book ▶ _on_ Saturday. Have you finished it already?
  Jolie: I read it _in_ about three hours yesterday.

1 Valerie: Will the bank be open .... nine-thirty?
  Cory: Yes, it always opens right .... time.

2 Preva: We're leaving .... two o'clock, and you haven't even changed.
  Glen: It's OK. I can easily shower and change .... ten minutes.

3 Cassidy: Your mother's birthday is .... Monday, isn't it?
  James: Yes, I just hope this card gets there .... time.

4 Madeline: If we ever go camping again, it's going to be .... the summer, not winter.
  Vance: Never mind. We'll be home .... two days, and then we'll be warm again.

Preposition + noun

1 Some useful phrases

on vacation, on business, on a trip/a tour
> *I'm travelling **on business**.*   *We're **on a** cycling **tour** of Europe.*

in cash, by cheque/credit card
> *It's cheaper if you pay **in cash**.*   *Can I pay **by credit card**?*

in writing, in pen/ink/pencil
> *Could you confirm that **in writing**?*   *I'll write the names **in pencil**.*

on television, on the radio/the phone/the Internet
> *I saw the movie **on TV**.*   *Mark is **on the phone** right now.*

for sale, on the market
> *The house next door is **for sale**.*   *It's the best stereo **on the market**.*

on the whole, in general
> ***On the whole** it's a good idea, but there are one or two problems.*
> *People **in general** aren't very interested in politics.*

in advance, up to date, out of date
> *The company wants us to pay for the goods **in advance**.*
> *Oh no! My passport is **out of date**.*   *These latest figures are **up to date**.*

in my opinion, from my point of view
> *Curling is boring, **in my opinion**.*
> *Mathieu never sees things **from Yvette's point of view**.*

on purpose, by mistake/chance/accident
> *I didn't spill my drink **on purpose**.*   *I pressed the wrong button **by mistake**.*
> *We didn't plan to meet. We met **by chance** on the street.*

2 Way and end

On the way = during the trip. *I'm driving into town. I'll get some gas **on the way**.*	**In the way** = blocking the way *We couldn't get past because there was a parked car **in the way**.*
In the end = finally, after a long time *It took Claire hours to decide. **In the end** she chose a long blue dress.*	**At the end** = when something stops *We all left quickly **at the end** of the meeting.*

3 Transportion

We use **by** without **a/the** when we talk about a means of transportion.
> *We decided to go to Calgary **by train**.* NOT ~~go by the train~~

We can also use **in** and **on**.
> *It'll be quicker to go **in the car**.*   *Gaston got **on the train**.*

Note that **on foot** means "walking."
> *We came all the way **on foot**.* NOT ~~by foot~~

BY:	air, bicycle/bike, boat, bus, car, ferry, helicopter, hovercraft, plane, rail, ship, streetcar, subway, taxi, train
IN:	the/my/your car, a helicopter, a taxi
ON:	my bicycle/bike, the boat, the bus, the ferry, the hovercraft, the plane, the ship, the streetcar, the subway, the train

Practice

A Preposition + noun (1–2)

Write *by*, *from*, *in*, or *on*.

▶ There's something I want to listen to ..on.. the radio.

1 They've promised me more money, but I don't have it .... writing.

2 Why can't you look at the problem .... my point of view?

3 Would you mind moving? You're kind of .... the way here.

4 I dialed the wrong number .... mistake.

5 I booked our seats more than a month .... advance.

6 Sabine's cellphone was stolen while she was away .... a business trip.

7 Could you be quiet for a minute, please? I'm .... the phone.

8 We've had a few nice days, but .... general it's been a cold summer.

9 I was lucky. I found the solution .... accident.

10 It's a long drive. Let's stop somewhere .... the way and have lunch.

11 I spent hours looking for a hotel. .... the end I found one.

12 Are you here .... vacation or .... business?

B Preposition + noun (1–2)

What would you ask? Use the word in parentheses with the correct preposition.
You may also need to use *the* or *your*.

▶ Ask if you can reserve a room before you travel. (advance)
Can I reserve a room in advance?

1 Ask if you can pay in cash. (cash)
Can ....

2 Ask if the information is current. (date)
Is ....

3 Ask your friend if he dropped the ball deliberately. (purpose)
Did ....

4 Ask if there is anything to watch tonight. (television)
Is ....

5 Ask your teacher if he or she will be here on the last day of July. (end)
Will ....

6 Ask Meagan if she thinks nuclear power is a good idea. (opinion)
Is ....

7 Ask Nigel if he is selling his car. (sale)
Is ....

8 Ask Sarit if she approves of the plan in general. (whole)
Do ....

C Transportion (3)

Complete the conversation. Write *by*, *in*, or *on*.

Kim: It's a long way to Montreal. Why don't you go (▶) ..on.. the train?

Courtland: I don't know. I think I'd rather go (1) .... car.

Kim: How far is your hotel from the train station?

Courtland: Oh, it's only five minutes (2) .... foot, but with all my luggage,
I'd probably go (3) .... a taxi.

Kim: Well, why not? It's more relaxing going (4) .... train, isn't it?

Courtland: I could go (5) .... air. That would be quickest.

Prepositional verbs

1 Introduction

A prepositional verb is a verb + preposition.

>*I'm **waiting for** you.   The dog **belongs to** our neighbours.*

The preposition always goes before the object.

>NOT *~~I'm waiting you for.~~*

In questions the preposition usually goes at the end of the sentence.

>*Who are you waiting **for**?*

Some verbs can go with a number of different prepositions.

>*I'm **looking at** these photos. They're really good.   I'm **looking for** my ticket. I can't find it anywhere.*
>*I'm **looking after** the children while their parents are out.   The police are **looking into** the matter.*

2 Some common prepositional verbs

Here are some more examples.

>*Yes, I **agree with** you.*
>*I **approve of** the new plan.*
>*Have you **applied for** the job?*
>*Do you **believe in** ghosts?*
>*Lots of people **care for** elderly relatives. (= look after)*
>*I didn't **care for** the movie. (= like)*
>*The US **consists of** fifty states.*
>*Giovanna finally **decided on** a vacation in Cuba.*
>*Whether we go out will **depend on** the weather.*
>*Everyone **laughed at** the joke.*
>*Did you **pay for** the coffee?*

>*I'll **see to** the matter at once.*
>*Donald's neighbours **apologized for** the noise.*
>*I think it's a good idea.*
>*The patient **asked for** a glass of water.*
>*I'm sorry, but I don't **care about** your problems.*
>*Please **concentrate on** your work.*
>*I can **deal with** any inquiries.*
>*I **feel like** a drink. (= want)*
>*I was **listening to** the radio.*
>*You can't **rely on** the weather forecast.*
>*Vicky **suffers from** headaches.*

We do not normally use a preposition after these verbs:
answer, approach, control, enter, leave, reach, request

>*The prime minister is **entering** the building.* NOT *~~He is entering into the building.~~*

3 About, of, and to

We can use **about** after many verbs. Here are some of them:
ask, complain, dream, enquire, hear, know, learn, speak, talk, think, wonder

>*Did you **hear about** the accident?   Sanjay was **talking about** golf.*

We do not use **about** after **discuss**.

>*We **discussed** the problem.* NOT *~~We discussed about the problem.~~*

Note the meaning of **dream of, hear of,** and **think of**.

>*I'd never tell you a lie. I wouldn't **dream of** it.*
>*Who's Jeff Munro? ~ I don't know. I've never **heard of** him.*
>*Did you like the play? What did you **think of** it?*

We can **apologize to, complain to, talk to,** and **write to** a person.

>*I'm **writing to** my sister.   We **talked to** Erdem about classical music.*

We do not use **to** after **call**. (= contact by phone)

>*I'm **calling** the office.* NOT *~~I'm calling to the office.~~*

Practice

A Prepositions with look (1)

Complete the conversation between Tanya and her friend Olivia. Write *after*, *at*, *for*, and *into*.

Tanya: Did you say you were looking (▶) ..for. a nanny?

Olivia: Yes, I was just looking (1) .... this ad. We need someone to look
(2) .... our children.

Tanya: How much do nannies get paid?

Olivia: I'm not sure. I'll have to look (3) .... how much they charge.

B Some common prepositional verbs (2)

This is some news that Milania has received from an old friend. Write these verbs and add a preposition after each one: *agree*, *applied*, *ask*, *care*, *caring*, *concentrate*, *decided*, *pay*, *suffering*

I'm working in a hospital now. I (▶) ..applied..for. a nursing position last July and started in August.
The pay is good, although I had to (1) .... my uniform with my own money.
I might (2) .... a pay raise later this year. But I don't really
(3) .... the money. The work is the important thing. Of course it's very hard
work (4) .... the patients, and at the moment I'm (5) ....
a backache. But I knew it would be like this when I (6) .... a career in nursing.
I just try to forget the problems and (7) .... the job. I think it's a worthwhile
thing to do, and I'm sure you (8) .... me.

C Some common prepositional verbs (2)

Write the verbs and add a preposition if necessary.

Akeil and Jenny had accepted an invitation to Rob and Twilla's party. Jenny had to stay late at work
to (▶) .take.care.of. (take care) one or two things. Her boss really (1) .... (relies)
her. It's usually Jenny who (2) .... (deals) all the little problems. Jenny didn't
really (3) .... (feel) going to a party but thought she should keep Akeil company.
She decided to go straight to the party instead of going home first. She (4) ....
(reached) the house just after nine. Akeil was sitting in his car outside waiting for her. He was
(5) .... (listening) the radio. Jenny (6) .... (apologized)
being late. At the party Akeil talked to a strange woman who (7) .... (believed)
ghosts. Jenny met a man who kept (8) .... (laughing) his own jokes.
She managed to get away from him but couldn't avoid a woman who wanted to
(9) .... (discuss) house prices. Akeil and Jenny (10) ....
(left) the party early and drove home feeling exhausted.

D About, of, and to (3)

Complete the conversation. Write *about*, *of*, or *to*.

Jacques: Did you hear about my experience at the Quick Burger Café?

Maureen: No. And I've never heard (▶) ..of. the Quick Burger Café.

Jacques: Oh, it's downtown. I was just talking (1) .... Vivienne about it.
They took at least twenty minutes to bring me a burger. I don't call that quick. I complained
(2) .... the waitress, and she poured a can of pop over me.

Maureen: Really? She must have had a bad day.

Jacques: The manager wasn't there, so I've written (3) .... him to complain (4) ....
the service. It was terrible. I wouldn't go there if I were you.

Maureen: I wouldn't dream (5) .... going there. I hate those burger places.

Direct speech and reported speech

1 Direct speech

Look at these examples of direct speech.

*Jay: **I'm tired**.*

*Wasn't it Greta Garbo who said, "**I want to be alone**?"*

*"**But I don't love you, Sotiris**," replied Nicole.*

We can show that words are direct speech by
putting them in quotation marks (" "). See
page 121. Sometimes the words are put after the
speaker's name, in the script of a play or movie, for
example. In a picture we can put the words in a
speech bubble.

> Raul and I are getting married next month. I know we'll be happy together.

2 Reported speech

In reported speech we give the meaning of what was said
rather than the exact words.

*Jay says **he's tired**.*

*Wasn't it Greta Garbo who said **that she wanted to be alone**?*

*Nicole replied **that she didn't love Sotiris**.*

> The actress Marie Jose Rodriguez and stock broker Raul Chavez have announced that they are getting married next month. Marie Jose is sure they will be happy together, she told reporters.

In reported speech we often change the actual words, e.g. "**I'm** tired" → **he's** tired.
Sometimes the verb tense changes, e.g. *I **want*** → she **wanted***.

In reporting we use verbs such as **announce, answer, explain, mention, promise, reply, say, suggest, tell,
warn**. The most common of these are **say** and **tell** (see part 3). We can also report thoughts.
   *We **think** the meal was expensive.   Phil **knew** Rayissa wanted to be with someone else.*

When we report statements, we often use **that**, but we can sometimes leave it out.
   *You promised (**that**) you wouldn't be late.   Sarah was saying (**that**) there's a problem.*

3 Tell or say?

TELL	SAY
We use **tell** if we want to mention the hearer (the person spoken to).	When we do not mention the hearer, we use **say**.
*Kelly's boss **told her** she could leave early.*	*Kelly's boss **said** she could leave early.*
NOT ~~Kelly's boss told she could leave early.~~	NOT ~~Kelly's boss said her she could leave early.~~
*Bryan **tells me** he's ready.*	*Bryan **says** he's ready.*
We use **tell** without an indirect object (e.g. **her, me**) only in the expressions **tell a story, tell the truth**, and **tell a lie**.	We sometimes use **to** after **say**, especially when the words are not reported.
	*The boss wanted to **say** something **to** Kelly.*
	*What did Adrian **say to** you?*

Practice

A Reported speech (2)

Why are these people at the doctor's? What do they say is wrong with them?

▶ I get pains in my leg.   1 I can't sleep.   2 I've hurt my back.   3 I feel sick all the time.   4 I fell and hurt myself.

▶ She says *she gets pains in her leg.*

1 She says ....

2 He says ....

3 ....

4 ....

B Reported speech (2)

Who said what? Match the words to the people and report what they said.
If you can't match them, check the bottom of the page.

▶	Al Capone	a)	"The world needs more Canada."
1	Don Cherry	b)	"I think I'm a good Canadian, but I'm not the greatest Canadian."
2	Margaret Atwood	c)	"Finishing second means you are the first driver to lose."
3	Bono	d)	~~"Canada? I don't even know what street it's on."~~
4	Gilles Villeneuve	e)	"If you're not annoying somebody, you're not really alive."

▶ *Al Capone said he didn't even know what street Canada was on.*

1 ....

2 ....

3 ....

4 ....

C Tell or say? (3)

Write *tell* or *say*.

▶ All the experts *say* the earth is getting warmer.

▶ Did you *tell* Jean and Maxime how to find our house?

1 The sales manager is going to .... everyone about the meeting.

2 Manu, why don't you just .... what the problem is?

3 They .... they're going to build a new amusement park here.

4 What did Natalia .... about her vacation plans?

5 Could you .... me which way the train station is, please?

6 The company should .... its employees what's going on.

7 You shouldn't .... lies, you know, Geraldine.

8 Did you .... anything to Malik about the barbecue?

Zero and First Conditionals (Real Conditionals)

1 Introduction

Come on, Jacqui. **If** we **hurry**, we**'ll** catch the nine-thirty bus.

There's no rush, is there? **If** we **miss** it, there**'ll** be another one in fifteen minutes.

Gloria and Jacqui are talking about possible future actions. They may catch the bus, or they may miss it.

2 First Conditional: **If we hurry, we'll catch the bus**

IF-CLAUSE		MAIN CLAUSE	
If	+ SIMPLE PRESENT		+ will
If we	*hurry,*	*we*	*'ll catch the bus.*
If we	*miss it,*	*there*	*'ll be another one.*
If it	*doesn't rain,*	*we*	*'ll be having a picnic.*
If I	*don't practise my skating,*	*I*	*won't get any better.*

The verb in the if-clause (e.g. **hurry**) is in the Simple Present, not the future.
     NOT *If we'll hurry, we'll catch the bus.*
But we can use **will** in the if-clause when we make a request.
     If you'll just wait a moment, I'll find someone to help you. (= Please wait a moment ...)

We can use the Present Progressive (e.g. **are doing**) or the Present Perfect (e.g. **have done**) in the if-clause.
     If we're expecting visitors, we'll need to clean the apartment.
     If you've finished with the ketchup, I'll put it away.

The main clause often has **will**. But we can use other modal verbs (e.g. **can**).
     If you don't have a television, you can't watch it.
     If Ian jogs regularly, he might lose weight.
     If Malcolm is going to a job interview, he should wear a tie.

The if-clause usually comes first, but it can come after the main clause.
     If I hear any news, I'll call you./I'll call you if I hear any news.

3 More uses of the First Conditional

We can use First Conditionals in offers and suggestions.
     If you need a ticket, I can get you one.   If you feel like seeing the city, we can take a bus tour.
We can also use them in warnings and threats.
     If you keep doing that, you'll make yourself sick.   If you don't apologize, I'll never speak to you again.

4 Zero Conditional

We sometimes use the Simple Present in both clauses.
     *If you **heat** water, it **boils**.   If Curtis **has** any money, he **spends** it.*
     *If you **press** this switch, the computer **turns** on.*
This means that one thing always follows automatically from another.
Pressing the switch always results in the computer turning on.

Practice

A First Conditional (1–3)

Read the conversation and then choose the correct forms.

Brenda: Have you heard about the music festival?

Nancy: Yes, (▶) it's/it'll be good if Everyday Autumn are playing. They're a great band.

Brenda: Will you be able to go, Randy?

Randy: If (1) I ask/I'll ask my boss, he'll give me some time off work, I think.

Nancy: How are we going to get there?

Brenda: Well, if (2) there are/there'll be enough people, we can rent a van.

Nancy: I won't be going if (3) it's/it'll be too expensive.

Brenda: It (4) isn't costing/won't cost much if we all (5) share/will share the cost.

Randy: If (6) I see/I'll see the others later on tonight, (7) I ask/I'll ask them if they want to go.

B First Conditional (1–3)

Comment on the situations. Use *if* + the present tense + *will/can*.

▶ It might rain. If it does, everyone can eat inside.
   If it rains, everyone can eat inside.

▶ The children must not go near Jasper's dog. It'll bite them.
   If the children go near Jasper's dog, it'll bite them.

1 Mary Ellen might fail her driving test. But she can take it again.

2 The Leafs might lose. If they do, Jeff will be upset.

3 The office may be closed. In that case Henri won't be able to get in.

4 Gary may arrive a bit early. If he does, he can help Ernie get things ready.

5 The party might go on all night. If it does, no one will want to do any work tomorrow.

6 Anna may miss the train. But she can get the next one.

7 Is Jimmy going to enter the race? He'll probably win it.

C Zero Conditional (4)

Match the sentences and join them with *if*.

▶ You lose your credit card.   I can't sleep.
1 You get promoted.   You get a warning letter.
2 I drink coffee late at night.   ~~You have to call the bank.~~
3 You don't pay the bill.   Your salary goes up.
4 I try to run fast.   The alarm goes off.
5 Someone enters the building.   I run out of breath.

▶ *If you lose your credit card, you have to call the bank.*
1
2
3
4
5

First and Second Conditionals
(Real and Unreal Conditionals)

1 Introduction

Carmella: *Would you like some pie, Melinda?*
Melinda: *No thanks. **If** I **ate** pie, I**'d** get fat.*
Carmella: *But it's delicious.*
Melinda: *It looks delicious. **If** I **had** your figure, I**'d** eat the whole thing.*

I ate pie and *I had your figure* are imaginary or unreal situations.
Melinda isn't going to eat the pie, and she doesn't have a figure like Carmella's.

2 Second Conditional (Unreal Conditional): **If I ate pie, I'd get fat**

IF-CLAUSE				MAIN CLAUSE
If	+	SIMPLE PAST	+	would
If I		**ate** pie,	I	'd get fat.
If I		**had** your figure,	I	'd eat the whole thing.
If we		**didn't have** a car,	we	'd find it difficult to get around.
If Tyra		**got** up earlier,	she	wouldn't always be late.

Note the Simple Past (e.g. **ate**). We do not use **would** in the if-clause. NOT ~~If I'd eat pie.~~
But we can use **would** in the if-clause when we make a request.

*If you**'d** like to come this way, the doctor will see you now.* (= Please come this way ...)

As well as the Simple Past, we can use the Past Progressive (e.g. **was doing**) in the if-clause.

*If Jada **were playing** her stereo, it wouldn't be so quiet in here.*

The main clause often has **would**. We can also use **could** or **might**.

*If we had a calculator, we **could** figure this out a lot faster.*
*If Nadia worked harder, she **might** do even better in school.*

The if-clause usually comes first, but it can come after the main clause.

***If** I knew, I'd tell you./I'd tell you **if** I knew.*

3 First and Second Conditionals

Compare these examples.

First: *If you **have** a nap, you**'ll** feel better.*
Second: *If I **had** a million dollars, I**'d** probably buy a yacht.*

The present tense (**have**) refers to a possible future action, something which may or may not happen.
The past tense (**had**) refers to something unreal. *If I had a million dollars* means that I don't a million
dollars, but I am imagining that I have. Compare these examples.

First: *If we **take** the car, we**'ll** have to pay for parking.*
Second: *If we **took** the car, we**'d** have to pay for parking.*

Here both sentences refer to a possible future action. But in the Second Conditional, the action is less
probable. *If we took the car* may mean that we have decided not to take it.

We can use Second Conditionals in offers and suggestions.

If you needed a ticket, I could get you one.
If you felt like seeing the sights, we could take a bus tour.

The Second Conditional is less direct than the First Conditional. The speaker is less sure that you want to
see the sights.

Practice

A Second Conditional (1–2)

Comment on these situations. Use a Second Conditional with *would* or *could*.

▶ Mitchell is such a boring person because he works all the time.
You know, *if Mitchell didn't work all the time, he wouldn't be such a boring person.*

▶ You can't take a picture because you don't have your camera.
How annoying. *If I had my camera, I could take a picture.*

1 You can't look the word up because you don't have a dictionary.
I'm sorry. ....

2 You don't email your friends because you're so busy.
I've got so much to do. ....

3 You can't play baseball because your back is aching.
I'm sorry. ....

4 Corinne won't marry Marco because she doesn't love him.
Of course, ...

5 Eddie can't find the way because he doesn't have a map.
Eddie's lost, but ....

6 Ryan has so many accidents because he's so clumsy.
You know, ...

B First and Second Conditionals (1–3)

Complete the conversation. Write the correct form of the verb. You may need to use *will* or *would*.

Didier: I haven't forgotten your birthday, you know. If you like, (▶) *I'll reserve* (I/reserve) a table for Thursday at our favourite restaurant.

Arlene: My birthday is on Wednesday, Didier. You're playing basketball then, aren't you? If you cared about me, (1) .... (you/not/play) basketball on my birthday.

Didier: What's the difference? If (2) .... (we/go) out on Thursday, it'll be just the same. If (3) .... (I/not/play), I'd be letting the team down.

Arlene: Yes, I suppose (4) .... (it/be) a disaster if you missed one game. Well, if (5) .... (you/think) more of your friends than you do of me, you can forget the whole thing.

Didier: I just don't understand you sometimes, Arlene.

Arlene: If (6) .... (you/think) about it, you'd understand. And I think (7) .... (it/be) better if we forgot all about my birthday.

Didier: Don't be silly, Arlene. If you get into one of your bad moods, (8) .... (it/not/do) any good.

Arlene: If you were interested in my feelings, (9) .... (I/not/get) into a bad mood.

C First and Second Conditionals (3)

What does the if-clause mean? Write a sentence with *isn't* or *might*.

▶ If this room were tidy, I could find things.   *The room isn't tidy.*
▶ If we're late tonight, we can take a taxi.   *We might be late tonight.*

1 If the phone were working, I could call you.   ....

2 If it rains, can you bring the washing in?   ....

3 If Mike were here, he'd know what to do.   ....

4 If this spoon were silver, it would be worth a lot.   ....

5 If Jamie calls, can you tell her I'll call back?   ....

Second and Third Conditionals
(Unreal and Past Conditionals)

1 Introduction

Nigel: *How was your camping trip?*
Dino: *Well, it **would have** been OK*
*if it **hadn't rained** all the time.*
Bella: *If we**'d gone** two weeks earlier,*
*we**'d have** had better weather.*

If it hadn't rained and *if we'd gone two weeks earlier* are imaginary situations in the past.
It did rain, and they didn't go two weeks earlier.

2 Third Conditional (Past Conditional): **If we had gone earlier, we would have had better weather**

IF-CLAUSE			MAIN CLAUSE	
If	+ PAST PERFECT			+ would have
If we	**'d gone** earlier,	we	**'d have** had better weather.	
If Gaston	**had called** her,	Shauna	**wouldn't have** been so annoyed.	
If you	**hadn't made** that mistake,	you	**'d have** passed your test.	
If Jean-Paul	**had been** more careful,	he	**wouldn't have** fallen.	

Note the verb in the Past Perfect (e.g. **had been**). We do not use **would** in the if-clause.
NOT ~~If Jean-Paul would have been more careful, he wouldn't have fallen.~~

The main clause often has **would have**. We can also use **could have** or **might have**.
*If I'd had my cellphone yesterday, I **could have** contacted you.*
*We just caught the bus. If we'd stopped to buy a paper, we **might have** missed it.*

The short form **'d** can be either **had** or **would**.
*If you**'d** called me, I**'d** have come to see you.* (= If you **had** called me, I **would** have come to see you.)

3 The use of the Third Conditional

We use the Third Conditional to talk about things in the past happening differently from the way they really happened. This sometimes means criticizing people or pointing out their mistakes.
If you'd been a bit more careful, you wouldn't have cut yourself.
If Francisco had set his alarm clock, he wouldn't have overslept.
We can also use this structure to express regret about the past.
If I hadn't gotten sick and missed the interview, I might have gotten the job.

4 Second and Third Conditionals

Compare these examples.
Second: *If you **planned** things properly, you **wouldn't** get into a mess.* (You don't plan.)
Third: *If you **had planned** things properly, you **wouldn't have** gotten into a mess.* (You didn't plan.)
We can mix the Second and Third conditionals.
*If you **had planned** things at the beginning, we **wouldn't** be in this mess now.*
*If you **hadn't left** all these dirty dishes, the place **would** look cleaner.*
*If Emil were more sensible, he **would have** worn a suit to the interview.*
*If I **didn't have** all this work to do, I **would have** gone out for the day.*

Practice

A Third Conditional (1–3)

Complete the conversation. Write the correct form of the verb. Use the Past Perfect or *would have*.

Michel: Our team didn't play very well today.

Sam: We were awful. But if Jason (▶) ..had..taken.. (take) that easy breakaway,
(▶) .we would have won. (we/win).

Michel: We didn't deserve to win. It (1) .... (be) pretty unfair if the
Raiders (2) .... (lose).

Sam: Jason was terrible. My grandmother (3) .... (score) if
(4) .... (she/be) in his position.

Michel: And if our goalie (5) .... (not/be) asleep,
he (6) .... (not/let) those goals in.

Sam: If Braden (7) .... (not/be) injured when we needed him most,
(8) .... (it/be) different.

Michel: Yes, (9) .... (we/beat) the Raiders if (10) ....
(he/be) on the ice.

B Third Conditional (1–3)

Comment on each situation using a Third Conditional with *if*. Use *would have*, *could have*, or *might have*.

▶ In a bookstore yesterday, Daniel saw a book he really wanted. The only problem was that he didn't
have any money. Daniel would have bought the book if he had had any money.

▶ Billie Jean often goes to concerts at the arena, although not to every one. There was one on Saturday,
but she didn't know about it. Billie Jean might have gone to the concert if she had
known about it.

1 On Sunday the students had to eat their lunch inside. Unfortunately it wasn't warm enough to
eat outside. ....

2 There was a bomb scare last Tuesday. Gina wanted to fly to Rome, but she wasn't able to. The
airport was closed. ....

3 Larissa has only met Craig once, and it's possible she wouldn't recognize him. He passed her
yesterday, but he had sunglasses on. ....

4 Sharon has been very busy, and she hasn't watered her plants for weeks. As a result, they've died.
....

5 Aaron likes hockey, but he didn't have a ticket to the game last week, so unfortunately he wasn't
able to get in. ....

C Second and Third Conditionals (4)

Complete the conversations. Write the correct form of the verb.
Use the Simple Past, the Past Perfect, *would*, or *would have*.

▶ Logan: You look tired.
Brittany: Well, if .you.hadn't.woken... (you/not/wake) me up in the middle of the night,
I.wouldn't.be.... (I/not be) so tired.

1 Vera: Is Ivan a practical person?
Candace: Ivan? No, he isn't. If .... (he/be) practical,
.... (he/pave) his driveway sooner. It took him forever.

2 Doug: Why are you sitting in the dark?
Duncan: Let's just say that if .... (I/pay) my hydro bill last month,
.... (I/not be) in the dark now.

3 Xavier: Why are you so mad at me? All I did yesterday was play rugby.
Sandy: If .... (you/love) me, ...
(you/not/leave) me here all alone.

Review test

Choose the correct answer (a, b, c, d) and write a, b, c, or d, as in the example.
The correct answers are on page 135.

Words and sentences

1 We gave .... some smoked salmon.
a) at the visitors b) for the visitors c) the visitors d) to the visitors

Verbs

2 My friend .... the answer to the question.
a) is know b) know c) knowing d) knows

3 I'm busy right now. .... on the computer.
a) I work b) I'm work c) I'm working d) I working

4 Where .... the car?
a) did you park b) did you parked c) parked you d) you parked

5 At nine o'clock yesterday morning we .... for the bus.
a) wait b) waiting c) was waiting d) were waiting

6 When I looked into the nursery, the baby .... quietly.
a) is sleeping b) slept c) was sleeping d) were sleeping

7 Here's my report. .... it at last.
a) I finish b) I finished c) I'm finished d) I've finished

8 I've .... made some coffee. It's in the kitchen.
a) ever b) just c) never d) yet

9 My arms are aching now because .... since two o'clock.
a) I'm swimming b) I swam c) I swim d) I've been swimming

10 When Raul .... the car, he took it out for a drive.
a) had fixed b) has fixed c) fixed d) was fixing

11 Sun was out of breath because ....
a) she'd been running b) she did run c) she's been running d) she's run

12 Don't worry. I .... be here to help you.
a) not b) will c) willn't d) won't

13 Our friends .... meet us at the airport tonight.
a) are b) are going to c) go to d) will be to

14 Where's Roberto? .... a shower?
   a) Does he have b) Has he c) Has he got d) Is he having

Questions, negatives, and answers

15 What's the weather like in France? How often .... there?
   a) does it snow b) does it snows c) snow it d) snows it

16 I really enjoyed the club. It was great, ...?
   a) is it b) isn't it c) was it d) wasn't it

17 Are we going the right way? ~ I think ....
   a) indeed b) it c) so d) yes

Modal verbs

18 We had a party last night. .... spend all morning cleaning up the mess.
   a) I must have b) I've been to c) I've had to d) I've must

19 There was no one else at the box office. I .... in a lineup.
   a) didn't need to wait b) must not wait c) didn't need to have waited d) don't need to wait

Passive

20 We can't go this way because the road is ....
   a) been paved b) being paved c) pave d) paved

21 I'm going to go out and ....
   a) have cut my hair b) have my hair cut c) let my hair cut d) my hair be cut

The infinitive and the -ing form

22 The driver was arrested for failing .... an accident.
   a) of report b) report c) reporting d) to report

23 Someone suggested .... for a walk.
   a) go b) going c) of going d) to go

Nouns and articles (a/an and the)

24 I need to buy ....
   a) a bread b) a loaf bread c) a loaf of bread d) breads

25 My father is not only the town mayor, he runs ...., too.
   a) a business b) a piece of business c) business d) some business

26 The .... produced at our factory in Hamilton.
    a) good are b) good is c) goods are d) goods is

27 I was watching TV at home when suddenly .... rang.
    a) a doorbell b) an doorbell c) doorbell d) the doorbell

28 Our friends have a house in ....
    a) a West Vancouver b) the West Vancouver c) West Vancouver d) West of Vancouver

This, my, some, a lot of, all, etc.

29 Is that my key, or is it ....?
    a) the yours b) the your's c) your d) yours

30 Adrian has no interest in fashion. He'll wear ....
    a) a thing b) anything c) something d) thing

31 There's .... use in complaining. They probably won't do anything about it.
    a) a few b) a little c) few d) little

Pronouns

32 Let's stop and have a coffee. .... a café over there, look.
    a) Is b) It's c) There d) There's

33 The washing machine has broken down again. I think we should get ....
    a) a new b) a new one c) new d) new one

Adjectives and adverbs

34 The house was .... building.
    a) a nice old brick b) a nice brick old c) a brick old nice d) an old nice brick

35 This detailed map is .... the atlas.
    a) more useful as b) more useful than c) usefuller as d) usefuller than

36 We're really sorry. We regret what happened ....
    a) a bit b) much c) very d) very much

Prepositions

37 You can see the details .... the computer screen.
   a) at b) by c) in d) on

38 I've got a meeting .... Thursday afternoon.
   a) at b) in c) on d) to

39 This car is ...., if you're interested in buying it.
   a) for sale b) in sale c) at sale d) to sell

Verbs with prepositions and adverbs

40 I prefer dogs .... cats. I hate cats.
   a) from b) over c) than d) to

Reported speech

41 Someone .... the tickets are free.
   a) said me b) said me that c) told me d) told to me

Conditionals and **wish**

42 If .... my passport, I'll be in trouble.
   a) I lose b) I'll lose c) I lost d) I would lose

43 I don't have a ticket. If .... one, I could get in.
   a) I'd have b) I had c) I have d) I've got

44 If the bus to the airport hadn't been so late, we .... the plane.
   a) caught b) had caught c) would catch d) would have caught

Appendix 1: Word formation

A Introduction

Look at these examples.

> *Lots of people believe that God **exists**.*
> *Lots of people believe in the **existence** of God.*

Exist is a verb and **existence** is a noun. The word **existence** has two parts: **exist-** and **-ence**. We call **-ence** a "suffix." We add it to the end of the verb **exist** to form a noun.

We can also use suffixes to form verbs, adjectives, and adverbs.

> *The system is being **modernized**. (= made modern)*
> *I grew up in an **industrial** town. (= a town where there is a lot of industry)*
> *The man was behaving **strangely**. (= in a strange way)*

There are many different suffixes, such as **-ence**, **-ize**, **-al**, **-ly**, **-tion**, and **-ment**. Some of them can be used to form many different words. For example, there are a lot of nouns ending in **-tion**: **action, education, explanation, information, instruction**, etc. There are no exact rules about which suffix you can add to which word. Adding a suffix can also involve other changes to the form of a word.

> *industry → industrial   repeat → repetition   science → scientist*

Now look at these examples.

> *They're going to **play** the game on Wednesday.*
> *They're going to **replay** the game on Wednesday.*

We can add **re-** to the beginning of the verb **play**. We call **re-** a "prefix." A prefix adds something to the meaning of a word. The verb **replay** means "play again." We can also add prefixes to nouns and adjectives. See parts G and H.

B Noun suffixes

-ment	*the prospects for **employment** reach an **agreement***
-ion/-tion/-sion	*take part in a **discussion** increase steel **production** ask for **permission***
-ation/-ition	*an **invitation** to a party people's **opposition** to the idea*
-ence/-ance	*a **preference** for houses rather than condos a **distance** of ten kilometres*
-ty/-ity	*no **certainty** that we shall succeed keep the door locked for **security***
-ness	*people's **willingness** to help recovering from an **illness***
-ing	*enter a **building** reach an **understanding***

C Nouns for people

-er/-or	*the **driver** of the car a newspaper **editor***
-ist	*a place full of **tourists** a **scientist** doing an experiment*
-ant/-ent	*an **assistant** to help with my work **students** at the university*
-an/-ian	***Republicans** and Democrats the **electrician** rewiring the house*
-ee	*an **employee** of the company (= someone employed)*
	*notes for **trainees** (= people being trained)*

We also use **-er** for things, especially machines.

> *a hair **dryer**   a food **mixer**   a **blender***

D Verb suffixes

Many verbs are formed by adding **-ize** or **-ise** to an adjective. Some are formed by adding **-en**.

-ize	*European safety rules are being **standardized**. They **privatized** the company.*
-en	*They're going to **widen** the road here. I think this will **brighten** her day.*

E Adjective suffixes

Most of these adjectives are formed from nouns.

-al	*a **professional** musician Canada's **coastal** waters*
-ic	*a **metallic** sound a **scientific** inquiry*
-ive	*an **informative** guidebook an offer **exclusive** to our readers*
-ful	*a **successful** career feeling **hopeful** about the future*
-less	*feeling **hopeless** about the future (= without hope) **powerless** to do anything about it*
-ous	*guilty of **dangerous** driving **luxurious** vacation homes*
-y	*a **rocky** path the **salty** taste of sea water*
-ly	*a **friendly** smile a very **lively** person*
-able/-ible	*an **acceptable** error (= an error that can be accepted) a **comprehensible** explanation*
	*a **valuable** painting (= worth a lot of money) a **comfortable** chair*

F Adverbs

-ly	*He looked around **nervously**. I moved here very **recently**.*

G Some common prefixes

anti- (= against)	***anti-whaling** protestors **anti-government** troops*
inter- (= between)	*an **international** match **interstate** highways in the US*
mini- (= small)	*a **miniskirt** the **minibar** in your hotel room*
mis- (= wrongly)	***mishear** what someone says **miscalculate** the amount*
multi- (= many)	***multicoloured** lights a **multimillionaire***
over- (= too much)	*a tendency to **overeat** **overcrowded** roads*
post- (= after)	*the **post-war** world a **postgraduate** student*
pre- (= before)	***pre-game** entertainment in **prehistoric** times*
re- (= again)	*a **reunion** of old friends **reread** a favourite book*
semi- (= half)	***semi-skilled** work sitting in a **semicircle***
super- (= big)	*a huge new **superstore** a **supertanker** carrying oil*
under- (= too little)	*thin and **underweight** **underpaid** work*

H Negative prefixes

We can also use a prefix to form an opposite. For example, the opposite of **clear** is **unclear** (= not clear).
Un- is the most common negative prefix.

dis-	*a **dishonest** way to behave can't help being **disorganized** **dislike** the idea*
	***disappear** from the scene a **disadvantage** of the plan*
il- (+ l)	*an **illegal** drug an **illogical** answer*
im- (+ m or p)	*an **impossible** task an **impolite** question*
in-	*an **indirect** route the **invisible** man a great **injustice***
ir- (+ r)	*an **irregular** shape an **irrelevant** remark*
non-	***non-alcoholic** drinks a **non-stop** flight*
un-	*an **uncomfortable** chair an **unusual** event an **undated** letter*
	***uncertain** what to do **unpack** your suitcase **unzip** the bag*

Appendix 2: The spelling of endings

A Plural nouns

We add -s to a noun to form the plural.

a car → two cars   *a name → some names*

1   After -s, -sh, -ch, and -x we add -es /ɪz/.

glass → glasses   *dish → dishes*
match → matches   *box → boxes*

2   A few nouns ending in -o have -es.

heroes   potatoes   tomatoes

But most have s.

kilos   photos   pianos
stereos   studios   zoos

3   When a noun ends in a consonant + -y, the -y changes to -ies.

penny → pennies   story → stories

We do not change -y after a vowel.

day → days   alley → alleys

B The Simple Present -s ending

In the third person singular, a Simple Present verb ends in -s.

I know → he knows   I work → she works

1   After -s, -sh, -ch and -x we add -es /ɪz/.

pass → passes   wash → washes
catch → catches   mix → mixes

2   Some verbs ending in -o have -es.

go → goes /gəʊz/   do → does /dʌz/

3   When a verb ends in a consonant + -y, the -y changes to -ies.

hurry → hurries   copy → copies

We do not change -y after a vowel.

stay → stays   enjoy → enjoys

C The -ed ending

Most verbs have -ed in the past tense. Most past participles also end in -ed.

look → looked   call → called

1   If the verb ends in -e, we add -d.

hope → hoped   save → saved

2   When a verb ends in a consonant + -y, the -y changes to -ied.

hurry → hurried   copy → copied

3   Sometimes we double a final consonant. This happens when a one-syllable verb ends with one vowel and one consonant, e.g. *beg, plan.*

beg → begged   plan → planned

For more details about doubling, see part G.

D The -ing form

1   We normally leave out -e when we add -ing to a verb.

take → taking   drive → driving

But we keep a double e before -ing.

see → seeing   agree → agreeing

2   When a verb ends in -ie, it changes to -ying.

die → dying   lie → lying

But -y does not change.

hurry → hurrying

3   Sometimes we double a final consonant. This happens when a one-syllable verb ends with one vowel and one consonant, e.g. *win, put.*

win → winning   put → putting

For more details about doubling, see part G.

E Adverbs

We form many adverbs from an adjective + -ly.

slow → slowly   calm → calmly

1   We do not leave out -e before -ly.

safe → safely   strange → strangely

But there are a few exceptions.

due → duly   true → truly
whole → wholly

2   When an adjective ends in a consonant + -y, the -y changes to -ily.

angry → angrily   happy → happily

An exception is *shy → shyly.*

3   When an adjective ends in a consonant + -le, the -e changes to -y.

probable → probably   sensible → sensibly

4   When an adjective ends in -ic, we add -ally.

automatic → automatically /ɔːtə'mætɪkli/
romantic → romantically /rəʊ'mæntɪkli/

But there is one exception.

public → publicly

F The comparison of adjectives

We form the comparative and superlative of short adjectives with **-er** and **-est**.

old → older, oldest
quick → quicker, quickest

1 If the adjective ends in **-e**, we add **-r** and **-st**.
late → later, latest   fine → finer, finest

2 When an adjective ends in a consonant + **-y**, the **-y** changes to **-ier** or **-iest**.
heavy → heavier, heaviest
lucky → luckier, luckiest

3 Sometimes we double a final consonant. This happens when a one-syllable adjective ends with one vowel and one consonant, e.g. *big, flat*.
big → bigger, biggest   flat → flatter, flattest
For more details about doubling, see part G.

G The doubling of consonants

1 When we add **-ed**, **-ing**, **-er**, or **-est** to a word, we sometimes double a final consonant. This happens when a one-syllable word ends with one vowel and one consonant, e.g. *stop, get, thin, sad*.
stop → stopped   get → getting
thin → thinner   sad → saddest

2 We do not double **-y**, **-w**, or **-x**.
play → played   new → newest
fax → faxing
We do not double when there are two consonants.
ask → asking   short → shortest
rich → richer
And we do not double when there are two vowels.
seem → seemed   shout → shouting
fair → fairest

3 The rule about doubling is also true for words of more than one syllable (e.g. *permit = per + mit*), but only if the last syllable is stressed.
per'mit → per'mitted
pre'fer → pre'ferring
We do not usually double a consonant when the syllable is unstressed.
'open → opened   'enter → entering
An exception is that in Canadian English **-l** is usually doubled, even if the syllable is unstressed.
travel → travelled

Appendix 3: Punctuation

A Period (.), question mark (?), and exclamation mark (!)

A sentence ends with one of these punctuation marks.

Period:	*It's cold today.*	*The office was closed.*	*Please be careful.*
Question mark:	*Who's that?*	*Did you see the show?*	*Could you wait, please?*
Exclamation mark:	*Oh, no! I don't believe it!*		

B Semi-colon (;)

We can use a semi-colon between two separate statements which are linked in meaning.
Jenna is a very kind person; she visits Sri in the hospital every day.
We could also use a period here.

C Colon (:)

We can use a colon before an explanation or before a list.
Vicky felt nervous: she hated the dark.
There wasn't much in the fridge: a couple of sausages, some butter, and half a bottle of milk.

D Dash (–)

A dash is informal. It is sometimes used instead of a colon or a semi-colon.
I'm having a great time—there's a lot to do here.
Marisol felt nervous—she hated the dark.

E Comma (,)

We often use a comma when we link two statements with **and**, **but**, or **or**.
Daniel was tired, and his feet were hurting.   *It's a really good camera, but I can't afford it.*
Note the two subjects in each sentence: *Daniel... his feet* and *It... I.* When there is only
one subject, we do not use a comma.
Daniel sat down and took his shoes off.

We can also use a comma when a sentence has a linking word like **when** or **although**.
When the office is busy, Marina has to work late.

Sometimes a comma can separate an adverb or a phrase.
Marina, unfortunately, has to work late.   *On busy days, Marina has to work late.*
Here the commas separate *unfortunately* and *on busy days.*

The rules about commas are not very exact. In general, commas are more likely
around longer phrases. With a short phrase there is often no comma.
On busy days Marina has to work late.   *Sometimes she has to work late.*

It is less usual to separate something at the end of the sentence.
Marina has to work late when the office is busy.   *She stayed late to get the work done.*
We do not usually put a comma before **to** expressing purpose.

We also use commas in a list of more than two. The last two are linked by **and**, often without a comma.
I went out with Rachel, Vicky, Emma, and Matthew. (Or *I went out with Rachel, Vicky, Emma and Matthew.*)

F Quotation marks (" ")

We put direct speech in quotation marks.

Tatiana said, "You haven't put those shelves up yet."   *"I haven't had time," replied Nikhil.*

We normally use a comma to separate the direct speech from the rest of the sentence.
The comma comes before the quotation mark. Quotation marks are also called "quotes."

Single quotation marks are sometimes used.

Tatiana said, 'You haven't put those shelves up yet.'

We can put quotation marks around titles.

Have you read the poem "The Divine Comedy"?

We often use quotation marks when we mention a word or phrase.

What does "punctuation" mean?   *She calls her work "performance art."*

G Hyphen (-)

We sometimes use hyphens in these structures.

Compound noun: *a six-pack of pop*
Compound expression before a noun: *an oven-ready meal*
Noun formed from a phrasal verb: *ready for take-off*
Noun + **-ing** form: *interested in rock-climbing*
Before the last word of a compound number: *a hundred and twenty-six people*
After some prefixes: *anti-aircraft guns*

The rules about hyphens are not very exact. For example, you may see a compound noun written as **phonecard**, **phone-card** or **phone card**. Hyphens are not very frequent in Canadian English. If you are unsure, it is usually safer to write two separate words.

H Apostrophe (')

Look at these examples.

Today we're going up to the cottage.   *Everyone is looking at Wilmer's car.*

We use an apostrophe (') in short forms, when there is a missing letter, e.g. **we're** (= we are). We also use an apostrophe with **s** to form the possessive of a noun, e.g. **Wilmer's car.**

I Capital letters

There are two capital letters (big letters) in this sentence.

*The boss said **I** could leave early.*

We use a capital letter at the beginning of a sentence and for the word **I**.

We also use a capital letter to begin the names of people, places, companies, etc.

Mark and Sarah   *Quebec City*   *Main Street*   *Parliament Hill*   *Research in Motion*

This includes the names of books, movies, magazines, etc. All the important words start with a capital letter.

A Fine Balance   *Away from Her*   *Macleans*

We also use a capital letter for days of the week, months of the year, holidays and festivals, historical times, nationalities, and most abbreviations.

Monday   *August*   *Easter*   *the New Year*   *the Industrial Revolution*
some Italian wine   *the UN* (= the United Nations)

Appendix 4: Pronunciation

A Key to phonetic symbols

VOWELS				CONSONANTS					
iː	feed	ʌ	cup	p	put	f	first	h	house
i	happy	ɜː	bird	b	best	v	van	m	must
ɪ	sit	ə	away	t	tell	θ	three	n	next
e	ten	ei	pay	d	day	ð	this	ŋ	song
æ	sad	əʊ	so	k	cat	s	sell	l	love
ɑː	car	ai	cry	g	good	z	zoo	r	rest
ɒ	dog	au	now	tʃ	cheese	ʃ	ship	j	you
ɔː	ball	ɔi	boy	dʒ	just	ʒ	vision	w	will
ʊ	put	ə	dear						
u	actual	eə	chair						
uː	fool	ʊə	sure						

B Stress

In books about English, the symbol ' is used before a stressed syllable, the part of the word which is spoken with greater force.

midnight /ˈmɪdnaɪt/   *about* /əˈbaʊt/   *exercise* /ˈeksəsaɪz/   *belonging* /bɪˈlɒŋɪŋ/

Here the syllables **mid**, **bout**, **ex**, and **long** are stressed. It is important to get the stress on the correct part of the word. Stressing a word incorrectly can make it difficult to understand.

Now look at these two sentences.

We want to **protest** */prəˈtest/ against experiments on live animals.*
We want to organize a **protest** */ˈprəʊtest/ against experiments on live animals.*

Protest as a verb is stressed on the second syllable. As a noun it is stressed on the first syllable. There are a number of words like this, e.g. **conflict**, **contrast**, **export**, **import**, **increase**, **insult**, **produce**, **progress**, **protest**, **record**, **suspect**, **transfer**. Sometimes a change of stress means a change of vowel sound.

Verbs: *produce* /prəˈdjuːs/, *progress* /prəˈgres/, *record* /rɪˈkɔːd/
Nouns: *produce* /ˈprɒdjuːs/, *progress* /ˈprəʊgres/, *record* /ˈrekɔːd/

We also use stress to show which are the important words in a sentence.

'Claire has a 'lovely 'house. She 'bought it last 'year. It's 'right in the 'centre of 'town.

Here the important words are **Claire**, **lovely**, **house**, and so on. We do not usually stress "grammatical words" like **a**, **she**, **the**, and **of**.

C Intonation

The voice usually falls or rises on the most important word in the sentence. This word is usually at or near the end of the sentence.

Claire has a lovely ↘ house.

Here the voice falls when saying **house**, which is the key word.

The symbol ↘ is used for a falling intonation and ↗ for a rising intonation.

Everything is more or less ↘ ready. (a statement)
Everything is more or less ↗ ready? (a question)

The voice usually goes down in a statement and up in a yes/no question. In general, a fall means that what we say is complete. A rise means that what we say is incomplete, or it needs an answer.

The voice often rises in the first part of a sentence and falls at the end.

If you don't ↗ *mind, I ought to be* ↘ *going.*

There is always a fall or rise on the important part of the message. Which word is the key word depends on the meaning. Compare these examples.

My friend is upset. She just failed her ↘ *exam.*
I passed my exam last summer, but my friend has just ↘ *failed hers.*
Lots of people have failed their exams. My ↘ *friend just failed hers.*

D Voicing

Sounds can be voiced or voiceless. Voiced sounds are like those you make when you sing. All the vowels and some of the consonants are voiced. Voiceless sounds are like those you make when you whisper. Some of the consonants are voiceless. Compare these sounds.

VOICED		VOICELESS	
/b/	*bill*	/p/	*pill*
/d/	*down*	/t/	*town*
/g/	*gold*	/k/	*cold*
/z/	*prize*	/s/	*price*

The voiceless sounds are /p/, /t/, /k/, /f/, /θ/, /s/, /ʃ/, /tʃ/, and /h/.

E The -s ending

We sometimes add the ending -**s** or -**es** to a word. For example, we can do this to form the plural or the possessive of a noun.

some chairs   the bushes   Mark's car   the woman's name

We can also add -**s** or -**es** to a verb.

It looks nice and sunny.   Eric watches football on Sunday afternoons.

The pronunciation of -**s**/-**es** depends on the sound which is before it. The ending is pronounced /s/ after a voiceless sound, /z/ after a voiced sound, and /ɪz/ after a sibilant sound.

Voiceless + /s/	*lips* /ps/	*gets* /ts/	*takes* /ks/
Voiced + /z/	*jobs* /bz/	*hides* /dz/	*bags* /gz/
	Laura's /əz/	*days* /eɪz/	*knows* /əʊz/
Sibilant + /ɪz/	*buses* /sɪz/	*loses* /zɪz/	*crashes* /ʃɪz/

For voiced and voiceless sounds see part D. The sibilant sounds are /s/, /z/, /ʃ/, /ʒ/, /tʃ/, and /dʒ/.

F The -ed ending

We add -**ed** or -**d** to a regular verb to form the past tense or past participle.

We all **walked** *home.   They've* **closed** *the gates.*

The pronunciation of -**ed** depends on the sound coming before it. The ending is pronounced /t/ after a voiceless sound, /d/ after a voiced sound, and /ɪd/ after /t/ or /d/.

Voiceless + /t/	*hoped* /pt/	*worked* /kt/	*increased* /st/
Voiced + /d/	*robbed* /bd/	*begged* /gd/	*raised* /zd/
	played /eɪd/	*allowed* /aʊd/	*cared* /eəd/
/t/ or /d/ + /ɪd/	*wanted* /tɪd/	*landed* /dɪd/	

For voiced and voiceless sounds see part D.

G Weak forms

We are using a weak form when we pronounce **is** as /s/ rather than /ɪz/, or we pronounce **from** as /frəm/ rather than /frɒm/. Normally a word like **is** or **from** is not stressed, and so we can use a weak form.

	STRONG FORM	WEAK FORM		STRONG FORM	WEAK FORM
a	/eɪ/	/ə/	*is*	/ɪz/	/z/ or /s/
am	/æm/	/əm/ or /m/	*me*	/miː/	/mi/
an	/æn/	/ən/	*must*	/mʌst/	/məst/ or /məs/
and	/ænd/	/ənd/, /ən/ or /n/	*of*	/ɒv/	/əv/ or /v/
are	/ɑː(r)/	/ə(r)/	*shall*	/ʃæl/	/ʃəl/ or /ʃl/
as	/æz/	/əz/	*she*	/ʃiː/	/ʃi/
at	/æt/	/ət/	*should*	/ʃʊd/	/ʃəd/
be	/biː/	/bi/	*some*	/sʌm/	/səm/ or /sm/
been	/biːn/	/bɪn/	*than*	/ðæn/	/ðən/
can	/kæn/	/kən/	*that*	/ðæt/	/ðət/
could	/kʊd/	/kəd/	*the*	/ðiː/	/ði/ or /ðə/
do	/duː/	/du/ or /də/	*them*	/ðem/	/ðəm/ or /əm/
for	/fɔː(r)/	/fə(r)/	*there*	/ðeə(r)/	/ðə(r)/
from	/frɒm/	/frəm/	*to*	/tuː/	/tu/ or /tə/
had	/hæd/	/həd/, /əd/ or /d/	*was*	/wɒz/	/wəz/
has	/hæz/	/həz/, /əz/ or /z/	*we*	/wiː/	/wi/
have	/hæv/	/həv/, /əv/ or /v/	*were*	/wɜː(r)/	/wə(r)/
he	/hiː/	/hi/ or /i/	*will*	/wɪl/	/l/
her	/hɜː(r)/	/hə(r)/ or /ə(r)/	*would*	/wʊd/	/wəd/, /əd/ or /d/
him	/hɪm/	/ɪm/	*you*	/juː/	/ju/
his	/hɪz/	/ɪz/	*your*	/jɔː(r)/	/jə(r)/

Notes on weak forms

1 (r) means that an -r sound is pronounced before a vowel. In the phrase **for a minute**, the words **for a** are pronounced /fəre/.

2 **A, an**, and **the** are normally spoken in their weak form.

3 **Some** does not have a weak form when it means "some but not all."

4 **That** normally has a weak form when it is a linking word, e.g. *I knew that* /ðət/ *it was true.* It does not have a weak form when it means something at a distance from the speaker, e.g. *Look at that* /ðæt/ *car.*

5 **There** normally has a weak form in a sentence like *There's* /ðəz/ *a bookstore in town.*
It does not have a weak form when it means "in that place," e.g. *The bookstore is over there* /ðeə/.

6 A verb does not have a weak form in a short answer with **yes**.
Are you tired? ~ Yes, I am /æm/.

Appendix 5: Irregular verbs

VERB	PAST TENSE	PAST/PASSIVE PARTICIPLE
arise	arose	arisen
be	was, were	been
bear	bore	borne
beat	beat	beaten
become	became	become
begin	began	begun
bend	bent	bent
bet	bet	bet
		betted
bind	bound	bound
bite	bit	bitten
		bit
bleed	bled	bled
blow	blew	blown
break	broke	broken
breed	bred	bred
bring	brought	brought
broadcast	broadcast	broadcast
build	built	built
burn	burned	burned
	burnt	burnt
burst	burst	burst
buy	bought	bought
catch	caught	caught
choose	chose	chosen
come	came	come
cost	cost	cost
creep	crept	crept
cut	cut	cut
deal /diːl/	dealt /delt/	dealt /delt/
dig	dug	dug
dive	dove	dived
	dived	
do	did	done
draw	drew	drawn
dream /driːm/	dreamed	dreamed
	dreamt /dremt/	dreamt /dremt/
drink	drank	drunk
drive	drove	driven
eat /iːt/	ate /et/	eaten /'iːtn/
fall	fell	fallen
feed	fed	fed
feel	felt	felt
fight	fought	fought

VERB	PAST TENSE	PAST/PASSIVE PARTICIPLE
find	found	found
flee	fled	fled
fly	flew	flown
forbid	forbad(e) /fə'bæd/	forbidden
forget	forgot	forgotten
forgive	forgave	forgiven
freeze	froze	frozen
get	got	gotten
give	gave	given
go	went	gone
grind	ground	ground
grow	grew	grown
hang	hung	hung
have	had	had
hear /hɪə/	heard /hɜːd/	heard /hɜːd/
hide	hid	hidden
hit	hit	hit
hold	held	held
hurt	hurt	hurt
keep	kept	kept
kneel	knelt	knelt
know	knew	known
lay	laid	laid
lead	led	led
lean /liːn/	leaned	leaned
leap /liːp/	leapt /lept/	leapt /lept/
	leaped	leaped
learn	learned	learned
leave	left	left
lend	lent	lent
let	let	let
lie	lay	lain
light	lit	lit
	lighted	lighted
lose	lost	lost
make	made	made
mean /miːn/	meant /ment/	meant /ment/
meet	met	met
mow	mowed	mown
		mowed

VERB	PAST TENSE	PAST/PASSIVE PARTICIPLE
pay	paid	paid
put	put	put
read /riːd/	read /red/	read /red/
ride	rode	ridden
ring	rang	rung
rise	rose	risen
run	ran	run
say /seɪ/	said /sed/	said /sed/
see	saw	seen
seek	sought	sought
sell	sold	sold
send	sent	sent
set	set	set
sew	sewed	sewn
		sewed
shake	shook	shaken
shine	shone	shone
shoot	shot	shot
show	showed	shown
shrink	shrank	shrunk
	shrunk	
shut	shut	shut
sing	sang	sung
sink	sank	sunk
sit	sat	sat
sleep	slept	slept
slide	slid	slid
smell	smelled	smelled
speak	spoke	spoken
speed	sped	sped
	speeded	speeded
spell	spelled	spelled
spend	spent	spent
spill	spilled	spilled
	spilt	spilt
spin	spun	spun
spit	spat	spat
split	split	split
spoil	spoiled	spoiled
spread	spread	spread
spring	sprang	sprung

VERB	PAST TENSE	PAST/PASSIVE PARTICIPLE
stand	stood	stood
steal	stole	stolen
stick	stuck	stuck
sting	stung	stung
stink	stank	stunk
	stunk	
stride	strode	stridden
strike	struck	struck
swear	swore	sworn
sweep	swept	swept
swim	swam	swum
swing	swung	swung
take	took	taken
teach	taught	taught
tear	tore	torn
tell	told	told
think	thought	thought
throw	threw	thrown
tread	trod	trodden
understand	understood	understood
wake	woke	woken
	waked	waked
wear	wore	worn
weave	wove	woven
	weaved	weaved
weep	wept	wept
win	won	won
wind	wound	wound
write	wrote	written

The verbs in this list are also irregular when they have a prefix, e.g. **overtake – overtook – overtaken, foretell – foretold – foretold.**

A few verbs have irregular Simple Present forms:

VERB	SIMPLE PRESENT
be	I **am**; you/we/they **are**; he/she/it **is**
do	he/she/it **does** /dʌz/
go	he/she/it **goes** /gəʊz/
have	he/she/it **has**
say	he/she/it **says** /sez/

Answer Key

Pages 2–3

A
1. determiner
2. verb
3. pronoun
4. adverb
5. pronoun
6. verb
7. adjective
8. preposition
9. linking word
10. adverb
11. determiner
12. adjective
13. linking word
14. noun

B VERB: is, loves
NOUN: Claire, café
ADJECTIVE: wonderful, old, romantic
ADVERB: madly, unfortunately, too
PREPOSITION: of, for, at
DETERMINER: a, their, some
PRONOUN: He, her, they
LINKING WORD: and, but, so

C
1. verb
2. noun
3. adjective
4. verb
5. noun
6. verb
7. verb
8. noun
9. adjective
10. verb

Pages 4–5

A
1. subject
2. verb
3. complement
4. adverbial
5. object
6. complement

B
1. e
2. a
3. c
4. d

C
1. Jeff likes football.
2. David had an accident.
3. We moved the piano.
4. Teri is a tall woman.
5. Everyone sat on the floor.
6. Mike's friends gave him some help.

D
1. also, with several young people
2. first, in 2011
3. naturally, without help
4. fortunately, from the province

Pages 6–7

A
1. Tony gave Narmatha a sweater.
2. Grace gave Pierre a scarf.
3. Emma gave Matthew a tennis racquet.
4. Bob gave Carrie a necklace.

B
1. sold her bike to her sister.
2. told the joke to all his friends.
3. gave her neighbour some help.
4. wrote her teacher a letter.

C
1. for
2. to
3. to
4. for
5. for
6. to

D
1. them to the recycling bin.
2. me a job.
3. them to the police.
4. you my umbrella.

Pages 8–9

A
1. a feeling
2. a repeated action
3. a fact
4. a fact
5. a thought
6. a feeling
7. a repeated action
8. a thought

B
1. doesn't speak
2. walk
3. needs
4. love
5. doesn't eat
6. don't look
7. doesn't work
8. don't like
9. wins
10. don't own

C
1. I go
2. comes
3. we travel
4. don't you come
5. doesn't make
6. do you take
7. I love

8. does it cost
9. I don't know
10. that doesn't matter
11. I don't want
12. Does that annoy
13. it doesn't annoy
14. find

Pages 10–11

A
1. They're/They are playing basketball.
2. She's/She is taking a photo.
3. He's/He is painting a picture.
4. They're/They are carrying a package.

B
1. are trying
2. are you finding
3. is helping
4. We're/We are doing
5. We aren't/We're not spending
6. It isn't/It's not taking
7. are you waiting
8. I'm/I am finishing

C
1. it's/it is raining.
2. I'm/I am working.
3. you're/you are sitting on my coat.
4. I'm/I am writing an important letter.
5. I'm/I am getting/feeling better.

Pages 12–13

A
1. She swam in the ocean.
2. She had a picnic.
3. She played volleyball.
4. She went out dancing.

B
1. were
2. started
3. saw
4. called
5. tried
6. was
7. arrived
8. fought
9. brought
10. entered
11. found

C
1. We didn't try
2. did you see
3. I didn't know
4. did you go
5. I didn't like
6. did Sarah enjoy
7. I didn't want

ANSWER KEY • PAGE 127

Pages 14–15

A
1. were watching television
2. were dancing in the street
3. was driving his taxi
4. was writing an essay

B
1. were you doing
2. I was taking
3. She was coming
4. I was going
5. You weren't looking
6. you were going

C
1. I was making phone calls all evening.
2. I was waiting in the rain for half an hour.
3. I was making sandwiches all afternoon.
4. I was sitting in a traffic jam for two hours.
5. My neighbour was playing loud music all night.

Pages 16–17

A
1. She's/She has fixed it.
2. I've/I have opened the window.
3. They've/They have arrived.
4. He's/He has moved it.
5. We've/We have watched all these.

B
1. He's/He has broken his leg.
2. They've/They have built a house.
3. They've/They have seen a movie.
4. She's/She has caught a fish.

C
1. I haven't done
2. hasn't made
3. You haven't put
4. I've/I have hurt
5. you've/you have had
6. have you put
7. It's/It has disappeared
8. I've/I have looked
9. have you done
10. I've/I have painted
11. I've/I have cleaned
12. We've/We have made
13. has that brush gone
14. you've/you have left

Pages 18–19

A
1. just cleaned it.
2. He's/He has just made some/it.
3. I've/I have just eaten it.
4. she's/she has just checked them.
5. I've/I have just called her.

B
1. I haven't started it yet.
2. I've/I have just seen Andrew
3. he's/he has already finished
4. I haven't finished my outline yet.
5. You've/You have already begun
6. We've/We have already spent
7. I haven't done any real work yet
8. I've/I have just realized
9. I've/I have just decided

C
1. He hasn't had any fun for a long time.
2. He's/He has had a cold for a week.
3. He hasn't seen his friends for weeks.
4. He hasn't played any sports since last year.
5. He's/He has been busy with his classes for months.

D
1. called her since
2. seen them for
3. watched one for
4. had one since
5. played (it) since

Pages 20–21

A
1. been
2. been
3. gone

B
1. Have you ever been to San Francisco?
   No, I've never been to San Francisco
   I've been to Los Angeles.
2. Have you ever played basketball?
   No, I've never played basketball
   I've played volleyball.
3. Have you ever seen/read (the play) *Hamlet*?
   No, I've never read/seen *Hamlet*
   I've read/seen *Macbeth*.

C
1. the second time I've lost my debit card.
2. This is the third time the washing machine has broken down.
3. This is the first time I've been in/to Costa Rica.
4. This is the second time I've stayed in this hotel.
5. This is (about) the fifth time I've missed the bus.

D
1. I haven't seen her today.
2. we haven't been there this weekend.
3. we haven't had one this semester.
4. has called this evening.

Pages 22–23

A
1. have you been doing
2. She's/She has been helping
3. have you been studying
4. I've/I have been trying
5. it's/it has been getting

B
1. they've/they have been arguing
2. he's/he has been cooking
3. he's/he has been driving
4. He's/He has been waiting

C
1. Matthew has been swimming for an hour.
2. My friends have been travelling (around the world) for three months.
3. Antonello has been working for ten hours.
4. Celine and Rita have been talking for forty minutes.
5. Travis has been reading the book for a long time.

Pages 24–25

A
1. b
2. a
3. a
4. b

B
1. The train had just left.
2. The rain had stopped.
3. I'd/I had forgotten my ticket.
4. They'd/They had stolen it a week before.
5. I hadn't seen her for months.
6. I'd/I had just cleaned it.
7. I'd/I had already eaten my sandwiches.

C
1. had left
2. 've/have read
3. 've/have eaten
4. 'd/had ordered
5. 've/have made
6. had told
7. 'd had/had had
8. 's/has started
9. 've/have turned
10. 'd/had made

Pages 26–27

A
1. I'd/I had been working
2. I hadn't been looking
3. she'd/she had been dealing

4 I'd/I had been waiting
5 I'd/I had been reading

B 1 She'd/She had been crying.
2 He'd/He had been driving too fast.
3 They'd/They had been playing with matches.
4 He'd/He had been standing under a tree.

C 1 had been watching
2 'd/had been playing, hadn't won
3 'd/had been walking, 'd/had walked
4 'd/had stopped, was smoking
5 has been aching
6 was lying, 'd/had bought, 'd/had been reading

Pages 28–29

A 1 I'll be leaving here at the end of the month.
2 Luckily, they'll find an apartment for me.
3 The training program finishes next summer.
4 They'll decide about that next year.

B 1 future
2 future
3 future
4 future
5 present

C 1 a
2 a
3 b
4 b
5 a

Pages 30–31

A 1 future
2 decision
3 future
4 decision
5 future

B 1 I'll answer it/the phone.
2 I'll have (the) chicken (, please).
3 I'll carry the/your bag (for you).
4 I'll mail it/the letter (for you).

C 1 Josh will watch the game.
2 Linda's party will be fun.
3 Claude won't put up the shelves.
4 Gicela will be annoyed.

5 Alejandro will study all weekend.
6 Heather won't do any work.

D 1 will
2 Shall
3 will
4 will
5 will
6 Shall

Pages 32–33

A 1 He's/He is going to light the firework.
2 She's/She is going to hit the ball.
3 They're/They are going to catch a bus.
4 She's/She is going to answer the phone.

B 1 I'm/I am going to lend
2 He's/He is going to take
3 It's/It is going to be
4 is he going to keep
5 are we going to get
6 He's/He is going to have
7 We're/We are going to get
8 it isn't going to get

C 1 I'm/I am going to get wet.
2 I'm/I am going to be sick.
3 I'm/I am going to lose.
4 It's/It is going to crash!
5 It isn't going to stop.

Pages 34–35

A 1 She's/She has got a map. OR She has a map.
2 He hasn't got an umbrella. OR He doesn't have an umbrella.
3 They've/They have got a rabbit. OR They have a rabbit.
4 They haven't got a car. OR They don't have a car.

B 1 Has … got
2 hasn't got
3 didn't have
4 didn't have
5 haven't got

C 1 we're/we are having
2 you've/you have got OR you have
3 it hasn't got OR it doesn't have
4 Did you have
5 I had
6 Have you got OR Do you have

7 have
8 I didn't have

Pages 36–37

A 1 offering
2 making a suggestion
3 asking for information
4 requesting
5 inviting
6 asking for information
7 asking permission

B 1 Are you a rich man?
2 Are quiz shows your only hobby?
3 Did you work hard in school?
4 Have you got/Do you have any other interests?
5 Is it an interesting life?
6 Does your wife ask you quiz questions?
7 Do you answer questions in your dreams?

C 1 Are you going to Mexico?
2 Does Laura play tennis?
3 Did you enjoy your holiday?
4 Shall we (both) go for a walk?
5 Will you be at the club tonight?
6 Is the train on time?
7 Do Sam and Kathryn go camping?
8 Could I/Can I/May I borrow your squash racquet?
9 Do you have a motorcycle?

Pages 38–39

A 1 Yes, I can
2 Yes, it is
3 No, he hasn't
4 Yes, I did
5 No, they aren't
6 Yes, I do
7 No, he isn't
8 No, I haven't

B 1 No, we won't 5 Yes, she does
2 Yes, I did 6 No, we aren't
3 Yes, she has 7 No, we can't
4 No, I didn't 8 No, I'm/I am not
5 Yes, she does
6 No, we aren't
7 No, we can't

C 1 b
2 b
3 b
4 a
5 b
6 a
7 b
8 b

Pages 40–41

A
1. a comment
2. a comment
3. a question
4. a question

B
1. isn't it?
2. are there?
3. aren't you?
4. didn't you?
5. don't they?
6. can't we?
7. was it?

C
1. don't you?
2. haven't I?
3. aren't you?
4. do you?
5. does it?
6. is there?
7. can you?

D
1. Let's listen to some music, shall we?
2. You don't have a train timetable, do you?
3. Pass me the salt, can you?/could you? OR You couldn't pass me the salt, could you?

Pages 42–43

A
1. neither am I
2. Neither can I
3. so am I
4. so do I
5. Neither do I
6. so would I

B
1. neither does Riyaad.
2. so has Riyaad.
3. neither can Akeil.
4. neither is Emili.
5. so does Riyaad.
6. so does Jenny.

C
1. I don't expect so
2. I suppose so
3. I hope not
4. I don't think so
5. I'm afraid not

Pages 44–45

A (Can, could, and may are all possible.)
1. Can I borrow your calculator?
2. May I join you?
3. Could I look at your notes?

B
1. You can have a picnic.
2. You can't drop litter.
3. You can turn left.

4. You can't play ball games/soccer.
5. You can't smoke.

C
1. I wasn't allowed to have
2. we're/we are allowed to have
3. we're/we are allowed to do
4. we'll/we will be allowed to have

D
1. Am I allowed to
2. May I
3. Am I allowed to
4. Am I allowed to
5. May I

Pages 46–47

A
1. I had to pay, did you have to pay
2. You have to slam, You'll have to fix
3. do you have to take, I'll have to take
4. We had to move, We didn't have to look, We've/We have had to do
5. has to start, does he have to get

B
1. "You must get to work on time."
2. has to keep his dog under control.
3. "You must listen carefully."
4. visitors have to report to the security officer.

C
1. must
2. has to
3. have to
4. must
5. have to
6. must
7. must

Pages 48–49

A
1. must, must not, don't need to
2. must not, must
3. must not, don't need to
4. must not, must, don't need to

B
1. didn't have to wait forever to cross the road.
2. don't have to work long hours.
3. doesn't have to work in a factory.
4. didn't have to lock their doors.
5. don't have to wash their clothes by hand.

C
1. must not
2. doesn't have to
3. must
4. don't need to, must not
5. must, doesn't have to

Pages 50–51

A
1. Dinner is being served.
2. Some houses are being built.
3. The seals are being fed.
4. A flag is being raised.

B
1. is owned
2. was being used
3. was leased
4. hadn't been looked
5. has been done
6. is used

C
1. will be done/are going to be done
2. will … be called
3. can't be bought
4. should be sold

D
1. got hurt
2. get lost
3. get broken
4. got divorced

Pages 52–53

A
1. had his car fixed.
2. is having her photo taken.
3. had his windows cleaned.
4. is having her eyes tested.

B
1. Diego (has) had his arm bandaged.
2. Craig is going to have his cavity filled.
3. Rose is having her photos developed.

C
1. did you get your arm bandaged, Diego?
2. did you get your cavity filled, Craig?
3. did you get your photos developed, Rose?

D
1. Jacob had his car stolen from outside his house.
2. Rita had her rent increased by ten percent.
3. David has had his hydro cut off.

Pages 54–55

A
1. Wayne promised to mow the lawn (soon).
2. Kathryn decided to buy both dresses.
3. Kim offered to cook dinner.
4. Ken threatened to give Nick an extra assignment.

B
1. They seem to believe
2. it seems to have improved
3. She doesn't seem to like

4 He seems to be working
5 He doesn't seem to be taking

C 1 to hang
2 to come
3 to be having
4 to invite
5 to take
6 to have left

Pages 56–57

A 1 I've/I have given up trying.
OR I gave up trying.
2 I can't imagine being
3 I enjoy watching it on TV.
4 suggested having a party.

B 1 can't stand lying
2 couldn't/can't resist having
3 couldn't face doing
4 can't help feeling

C 1 trying
2 walking
3 calling
4 waiting
5 getting
6 changing
7 missing
8 discussing

Pages 58–59

A 1 uncountable
2 countable
3 countable
4 uncountable
5 uncountable
6 uncountable
7 countable
8 countable

B 1 some cookies
2 a light bulb
3 some wine
4 some water
5 a banana
6 some soap
7 a lemon
8 some butter
9 some eggs

C 1 a laptop
2 essays
3 hours
4 many
5 money
6 food
7 much
8 a job
9 some
10 a few
11 pictures

Pages 60–61

A 1 a jar of jam
2 a box of matches
3 two loaves of bread
4 a bar of chocolate
5 five kilograms of potatoes
6 a box of breakfast cereal
7 two bottles of mineral water
8 a tube of toothpaste

B 1 some
2 some
3 some
4 a
5 some
6 some
7 a
8 some

C 1 beautiful scenery
2 good weather
3 dinner
4 fun
5 an awful trip

Pages 62–63

A 1 coffee
2 some apples
3 painting
4 a noise
5 cheese
6 a conversation
7 some chicken
8 war
9 life
10 some egg

B 1 some business
2 an iron
3 a glass, a light
4 a business, some time
5 some experience, an experience

C 1 time
2 an experience
3 a painting
4 a paper
5 a mango
6 fruits

Pages 64–65

A 1 thanks
2 damages
3 pain
4 belongings
5 saving
6 goods
7 damage
8 savings
9 pains

B 1 mathematics
2 history
3 economics
4 geography

C 1 are
2 is
3 were
4 seem
5 is
6 were

D 1 was
2 outskirts
3 headquarters
4 savings
5 damage
6 aren't
7 is
8 gives

Pages 66–67

A 1 a
2 the
3 a
4 the
5 The
6 the
7 the
8 a
9 The
10 the
11 the
12 the
13 the
14 a
15 the
16 the
17 an
18 the
19 the
20 the

B 1 Matthew won the race easily.
2 Suddenly a child ran onto the road.
3 She was watching a movie on television.
4 The bus was half an hour late.
5 The camera recorded the thief.

C 1 a, the, the
2 a, the, a
3 the, the
4 a, the, The
5 a, the
6 a, the/a
7 a, the

Pages 68–71

A 1 Lake Michigan
2 Italy

3 The Andes
4 The Maritime Provinces
5 Tasmania
6 the West Indies
7 The River Nile
8 Mexico City
9 the South

B 1 the Don River
2 High Park
3 Billy Bishop Airport
4 Yonge-Dundas Square
5 Humber Bridge
6 Lake Ontario
7 the Royal Alex Theatre
8 the Annex neighbourhood
9 The Gardiner Expressway
10 The Ritz-Carlton

C 1 New York
2 the Statue of Liberty
3 Central Park
4 the Metropolitan Museum of Art
5 Broadway
6 Macy's
7 Washington Square
8 New York University
9 the Paramount
10 Broadway

D 1 the Museum of Nature
2 Elgin Street
3 the Rideau Canal
4 the Parliament Buildings
5 Quebec

E 1 is on Powerhouse Drive.
2 The RCMP Heritage Centre is on Dewdney Avenue.
3 The Mackenzie Art Gallery is on Albert Street.
4 Mosiac Stadium is on 10th Avenue.
5 The Conexus Arts Centre is on Lakeshore Drive.
6 The University of Regina is on Wascana Drive.
7 The Legislative Building is on Legislative Drive.

F 1 A day at Canada's Wonderland
2 A train trip through the Rockies
3 A tour of the White House
4 A beach on the Riviera
5 A shopping trip to West Edmonton Mall
6 A small town in France
7 A trip across the Golden Gate Bridge

8 A walk around Lake Winnipeg
9 A visit to the CN Tower
10 A hike across Newfoundland
11 A tour of the National Gallery
12 A boat trip along the Fraser River

Pages 72–73

A

	Near	Further away
Singular		that
Plural	these	those

B 1 these flowers
2 this package
3 those trees
4 dog...that

C 1 That
2 these
3 this
4 this
5 those
6 that
7 This
8 this, That
9 These

Pages 74–75

A 1 our
2 his
3 his
4 their
5 yours
6 mine
7 hers
8 her

B 1 its
2 it's
3 it's
4 its

C 1 the
2 her
3 the OR her
4 their
5 your, your

D 1 Jenny introduced me to a friend of hers.
2 They've got their own pool.
3 It's a favourite hobby of mine.
4 I've got some books of his.
5 I'd like my own room.

Pages 76–77

A 1 She has some cats.
2 He doesn't have any gas.
3 He has some poison.

B 1 any
2 any
3 some
4 some
5 some
6 any

C 1 some, anything
2 someone, any/some
3 anyone (or someone), any
4 something, some

D 1 anyone
2 any bus
3 any colour
4 anything
5 any day

Pages 78–79

A 1 She hasn't had many lessons yet.
2 I'll have to make a lot (of it).
3 I don't have much energy.
4 Maybe you should add a little water/a few drops of water.
5 We invited lots of friends/a lot of friends.

B 1 a lot of
2 many/a lot of
3 many
4 a lot of
5 much/a lot of
6 many/a lot of
7 much

C 1 few
2 little
3 a little
4 a few
5 little
6 a few

D 1 much
2 little
3 much
4 many
5 few
6 little

Pages 80–81

A 1 the shirt
2 Laura
3 the jeans
4 Christina
5 Christina and Garrick
6 Christina
7 Oscar and Miranda
8 Tom

B 1 he
2 them
3 us/me

4 her
5 she
6 she
7 them
8 she
9 They
10 you
11 him
12 he
13 you/we
14 him

C 1 We
2 you, us
3 it, it, her, She
4 Me, it
5 she, her
6 I, you, them, they

D 1 You
2 they
3 You
4 they

Pages 82–83

A 1 There's/There is a balloon in the sky.
2 There are some boxes on the car.
3 There's/There is an elephant in the garden.

B 1 There's/There is, There'll be
2 are there, There's/There has been OR There was
3 there was, There … have been

C 1 It was very cheap.
2 It was Jasmine.
3 It's/It is very inconvenient.
4 It's/It is very warm.
5 It's/It is important to keep it somewhere safe.

D 1 There
2 It
3 There, It
4 there, it
5 It, there, It, there

Pages 84–85

A 1 a formal one or a casual one, a casual one
2 a big one or a small one, A big one
3 A white one or a grey one, A grey one
4 a manual one or an electric one, a manual one

B 1 I don't have one.
2 I need to get some new ones.

3 Have you seen this one?
4 I've rented one.
5 Can't you find any nice ones?
6 The one in the car is better.

C 1 one
2 it
3 one
4 them
5 some

Pages 86–87

A 1 modern chairs
2 a black cat
3 solar power
4 classical music
5 an old car
6 a tall building

B beautiful, ideal, quiet, short, popular, scenic, friendly, helpful, good, amazing, excellent, local

C 1 The World is Asleep
2 My Chief Desire
3 My Heart is Content
4 The Main Thing to Remember
5 The Night is Alive
6 Inner Secrets
7 The Only Girl for Me

Pages 88–89

A 1 a small white car
2 an attractive old building
3 an expensive wooden garden bench
4 a famous Italian opera singer

B 1 a lovely old glass vase
2 an attractive wall mirror
3 a modern office desk
4 red metal kitchen chairs
5 an interesting old model boat
6 valuable Australian postage stamps
7 a small wooden coffee table

C 1 This is a powerful Japanese office computer.
2 This is a small electric energy-efficient fireplace.
3 This is a big new chocolate bar.
4 This is a terrific Canadian television show.
5 These are stylish aluminum garage doors.
6 These are wonderful new sports shoes.
7 This is a very good small Korean cellphone.

Pages 90–93

A 1 are more interesting
2 is higher
3 is more beautiful

B 1 most valuable
2 best
3 greatest
4 most exciting
5 most popular
6 most successful
7 most exciting
8 most loyal

C 1 happier
2 faster
3 more helpful
4 shinier
5 bigger
6 more restful
7 more modern

D 1 better
2 longer
3 more often
4 more carefully
5 earlier
6 louder/more loudly

E 1 worst
2 better
3 worse
4 best
5 furthest

F 1 least
2 less
3 more
4 Most

G 1 happier
2 smallest
3 best
4 shorter
5 most important
6 older
7 more exciting
8 most
9 wetter
10 lower
11 worse

Pages 94–95

A 1 She's very busy.
2 She's a bit thirsty.
3 He's very strong.
4 He's extremely happy.

B 1 very
2 pretty
3 a bit
4 very
5 a bit
6 pretty

C 1 That radio is a bit loud.
2 I absolutely love my new job.
3 Why don't you slow down a little?
4 The rain completely spoiled our day./The rain spoiled our day completely.
5 We did the job fairly quickly.
6 I feel a lot better now.
7 We enjoyed the concert very much. OR We very much enjoyed the concert.
8 My arms ached a lot.

D 1 absolutely
2 really
3 very much
4 extremely
5 very
6 totally
7 very

Pages 96–97

A 1 He's/He is on the roof.
2 They're/They are at the club.
3 He's/He is in the bath.
4 She's/She is at the intersection.

B 1 at the gas station
2 at the zoo
3 in the theatre
4 in the restaurant
5 at the station

C 1 in
2 on
3 in
4 at
5 at
6 at
7 on
8 on
9 in
10 in/at

Pages 98–99

A 1 In 1970.
2 On October 17, 1970.
3 In October.

B 1 X
2 on
3 X
4 in
5 at
6 on
7 in
8 in
9 on
10 at

C 1 in time
2 on time
3 in time
4 on time

D 1 at, on
2 at, in
3 on, in
4 in, in

Pages 100–101

A 1 in
2 from
3 in
4 by
5 in
6 on
7 on
8 in
9 by
10 on
11 In
12 on, on

B 1 I pay in cash?
2 the information up to date?
3 you drop the ball on purpose?
4 there anything (to watch) on television tonight?
5 you be here at the end of July?
6 nuclear power a good idea in your opinion?
7 your car for sale?
8 you approve of the plan on the whole?

C 1 by
2 on
3 in
4 by
5 by

Pages 102–103

A 1 at
2 after
3 into

B 1 pay for
2 ask for
3 care about
4 caring for
5 suffering from
6 decided on
7 concentrate on
8 agree with

C 1 relies on
2 deals with
3 feel like
4 reached
5 listening to

6 apologized for
7 believed in
8 laughing at
9 discuss
10 left

D 1 to
2 to
3 to
4 about
5 of

Pages 104–105

A 1 she can't sleep.
2 he's/he has hurt his back.
3 She says she feels sick all the time.
4 He says he fell and hurt himself.

B 1 Don Cherry said (that) he thinks he's a good Canadian, but not the greatest Canadian.
2 Margaret Atwood said (that) if you're not annoying somebody, you're not really alive.
3 Bono said (that) the world needs more Canada.
4 Gilles Villeneuve said (that) finishing second means you are the first driver to lose.

C 1 tell
2 say
3 say
4 say
5 tell
6 tell
7 tell
8 say

Pages 106–107

A 1 I ask
2 there are
3 it's
4 won't cost
5 share
6 I see
7 I'll ask

B 1 If Mary Ellen fails her driving test, she can take it again.
2 If the Leafs lose, Jeff will be upset.
3 If the office is closed, Henri won't be able to get in.
4 If Gary arrives a bit early, he can help Ernie get things ready.
5 If the party goes on all night, no one will want to do any work tomorrow.

6 If Anna misses the train, she can get the next one.

7 If Jimmy enters the race, he'll probably win it.

C 1 If you get promoted, your salary goes up.

2 If I drink coffee late at night, I can't sleep.

3 If you don't pay the bill, you get a warning letter.

4 If I try to run fast, I run out of breath.

5 If someone enters the building, the alarm goes off.

Pages 108–109

A 1 If I had a dictionary, I could look the word up.

2 If I wasn't so busy, I'd/I would email my friends.

3 If my back wasn't aching, I could play baseball.

4 if Corinne loved Marco, she'd/she would marry him.

5 if he had a map, he could find the way.

6 if he/Ryan wasn't so clumsy, he wouldn't have so many accidents.

B 1 you wouldn't play

2 we go

3 I didn't play

4 it'd be/it would be

5 you think

6 you thought

7 it'd be/it would be

8 it won't do

9 I wouldn't get

C 1 The phone isn't working.

2 It might rain.

3 Mike isn't here.

4 The/This spoon isn't silver.

5 Jamie might call.

Pages 110–111

A 1 would have been

2 had lost

3 would have scored

4 she'd been/she had been

5 hadn't been

6 wouldn't have let

7 hadn't been

8 it would have been

9 we'd have beaten/we would have beaten

10 he'd been/he had been

B 1 The students could/would have eaten their lunch outside if it had been warm enough/if it hadn't been so cold.

2 Gina could/would have flown to Rome if the airport hadn't been closed/had been open.

3 Larissa might have recognized Craig if he hadn't had sunglasses on.

4 Sharon's plants wouldn't have died/might not have died if she'd/she had watered them.

5 Aaron could/would have got in (to the hockey game) if he'd/he had had a ticket.

C 1 he was/were, he'd/he would have paved

2 I'd/I had paid, I wouldn't be

3 you loved, you wouldn't have left

Pages 112–115 (Review Test)

The number after each answer indicates the page number on which you can find information about that grammar point.

1 c 6
2 d 8
3 c 10
4 a 12
5 d 14
6 c 14
7 d 16
8 b 18, 20
9 d 22
10 a 24
11 a 26
12 b 30
13 b 32
14 d 34
15 a 36
16 d 40
17 c 42
18 c 46
19 a 48
20 b 50
21 b 52
22 d 54
23 b 56
24 c 58, 60
25 a 62
26 c 64
27 d 66
28 c 68
29 d 72
30 b 74
31 d 76
32 d 80
33 b 82
34 a 86
35 b 88
36 d 94
37 d 96
38 c 98
39 a 100
40 d 102
41 c 104
42 a 106
43 b 108
44 d 110

Index

a 66
    a *chicken* or *chicken*? 62
a bit 94
a few 78
a little 78
a lot 78
a lot of 78
about after a verb 102
adjectives 86–88
    + **one/ones** 84
    comparative and superlative
        90–92, 119
    suffixes 117
    word order 86, 88
adverbials 4
adverbs
    + adverb 94
    of degree 94
    -ly ending 117–18
    word order 94
advice 60
afraid
    + **so** 42
allowed to 44
already
    with the present perfect 18
an 66
answering questions 36, 38
any 76
anyone, anything, etc. 76
apostrophes (') 121
appear
    + to-infinitive 54
articles *see* **a** and **the** 66–70
at
    at the end 100
    place 96
    time 108

be
    Present Perfect 16
    Simple Past 12
be allowed to 44
be going to 32
been to and **gone to** 20
believe so 42
best 91
better 91
bit of *see also* **a bit** 60
by
    transportation 100

can
    permission 44
can't
    refusing permission 44
can't help + **-ing** form 56
capital letters 121
carry on + **-ing** form 56
clothes, etc. 64
colons (:) 120
commas (,) 120
comparative 90–93
    spelling 119
comparison of adverbs 91
complement 4
conditionals 106–10
consonant doubling 119
could
    permission 44
countable and uncountable
    nouns 58–62

dashes (–) 120
definite article *see* **the**
demonstratives (**this** etc.) 72
determiners 72–8
did
    in the Simple Past 12, 36, 42
didn't 12
didn't need to 48
direct and indirect objects 6
direct speech 104, 121
do
    in the Simple Present 8, 36,
        42
does
    in the Simple Present 8, 36,
        42
doesn't 8
don't
    in the Simple Present 8
    with a question tag 40
don't have to 48
don't need to 48
doubling of consonants 119

each
    + **one** 84
-ed ending 12, 16
    pronunciation 123
    spelling 118
elder, eldest 91

endings of words 116–17, 118–19
    spelling 118–19
-er, -est ending 90
    spelling 119
ever with the Present Perfect or
    Simple Past 20
every
    + **one** 84
exclamation marks (!) 120
expect so 42

fail + **to-infinitive** 54
farther, farthest 91
few 78
First Conditional 106, 108
for
    buy it for you 6
    with the Present Perfect 18
    with the Present Progressive 22
further, furthest 91
future 28–32
Future Passive 50

get
    get dressed etc. 50
    get something done 52
    passive auxiliary 50
going to (future) *see* **be going to**
gone to and **been to** 20
got 34
guess so 42

had 34
had been doing 26
had done 24
had got 34
had to 46
has 34
has been doing 22
has done 16
have 34
    action verb 4
    have something done 52
    meaning 'experience' 52
    Present Perfect 16
have and **have got** 34
have been doing 22
have done 16
have got 34
have got to 46
have something done 52

have to 46–48
he 80
her 74, 80
hers 74
him 80
his 74
hope not 42
hope so 42
how long 22
 + Present Perfect 18
hyphens (-) 121

I (pronoun) 80
idioms
 preposition + noun 100
 prepositional verbs 102
if 106–10
 with **any** 76
imperative
 question tags 40
in
 in the end, in the way 100
 place 96
 time 98
 transportation 100
indirect speech 104
infinitive 54, 56
information 60
-**ing** adjective
 -ing form 56
 spelling 118
 after a verb 56
intonation 122–23
 in question tags 40
irregular comparative and
 superlative forms 91
irregular verbs 125–26
it 80–82
 and **one** 4
 and **there** 82
item of 60
its 74
it's 74

just with the Present Perfect 18

keep (**on**) + -ing form 56
key to phonetic symbols 122

lately
 with the Present Perfect
 Progressive 22
least 91
less 91

let's
 with a question tag 40
little 78 *see also* **a little**
'**ll** (short form) 30
lots of 78 *see also* **a lot of**
-**ly** ending 117–18

manage + **to**-infinitive 54
many 78
may
 permission 44
me 80
means, etc. 64
mind
 + -ing form 56
mine 74
modal verbs
 in conditionals 106–10
 passive 50
more 90
most 90
much 78, 94
must
 necessity 46
must not 48
my 74

names of places and **the** 68–70
necessity: **must, have to, don't
 need to** 46–48
negative prefixes 117
negative questions
 Why don't we ...? 8
neither
 neither do I 42
never with the Present Perfect
 and Simple Past 20
news 60, 64
no
 after a question tag 40
 in short answers 38
nor 42
not
 I hope not 42
nouns 58–64
 + **to**-infinitive 54
 countable and uncountable
 58–60
 for people 116
 plural 118
 singular or plural? 64
 suffixes 116

object 4
object pronouns 80

of
 carton of milk 60
 dream of 102
 a friend of mine 74
offers
 in conditionals 106–08
on
 place 96
 time 98
 transportation 100
 on the way 100
one
 meaning people in general 80
 and **ones** 84
ones 84
order of adjectives 86, 88
order of words *see* word order
our, ours 74
own (*my own*) 74

parts of speech 2
passive 50, 52
 verb forms 50
Past Progressive 14
 and Past Perfect Progressive 26
Past Perfect 24
 in conditionals 110
 and Past Perfect Progressive 26
 and Present Perfect 24
Past Perfect Progressive 26
past/passive participle
 irregular 125–26
 in the passive 50
 in the perfect 16
 see also participles
periods (.) 120
permission: **can, may**, etc. 44
personal pronouns 80
phonetic symbols 122
phrases of time 98
piece of 60
place names and **the** 68–70
plural nouns
 plural-only 64
 spelling 118
position of adverbs 94
possessive forms
 my etc. 74
prefixes 117
prepositional verbs 102
prepositions 96–102
 + noun without **the** 100
 + object pronoun 80
 of time 98
 after a verb 102

Present Progressive 10
Present Perfect 16–20
    and Past Perfect 24
Present Perfect Progressive 22
    and Past Perfect Progressive 26
pronouns 80–84
    personal 80
pronunciation 122–24
punctuation 120–21

quantifiers 76–8
question marks (**?**) 120
question tags 40
questions
    yes/no questions 36
quotation marks (**""**) 121

reported speech 104
requests
    with a question tag 40

-s ending
    plural 118
    pronunciation 123
    in the Simple Present 8, 118
say
    and **tell** 104
Second Conditional 108–10
seem
    + **to**-infinitive 54
semi-colons (;) 120
sentence structure 4
shall
    future 30
she 80
short answers 38
short forms 30
Simple Past 12
    in conditionals 108
    irregular 125–26
Simple Present 8, 118
    in conditionals 106
since
    with the Present Perfect 18
    with the Present Perfect
        Progressive 22
singular or plural noun? 64
so
    I think so 42
    so do I 42
some
    and **any** 76
someone 76
something 76
somewhere 76

spelling of endings 118–19
stress 122
structure of sentences 4
subject 4
subject pronouns 80
suffixes 116
suggestions
    in conditionals 106, 108
    with question tags 40
superlative 90–93
    + **one/ones** 84
suppose so 42
sure and unsure (about the
    future) 28

tag questions *see* question tags
tell and **say** 104
tend + **to**-infinitive 54
tenses of the verb
    passive 50
that 72
    + **one** 84
the 66
    + **one** 84
    in place names 68–70
their, theirs 74
them 80
there
    there + **be** 82
    there is and *it is* 82
these 72
    + **ones** 84
they 80
    meaning people in general 80
think so 42
Third Conditional 110
this 72
    + **one** 84
    this week etc. with the Present
        Perfect and Simple Past 20
those 72
    + **ones** 84
till *see* **until**
time: *first time* etc. with the
    Present Perfect 20
time phrases 98
to
    write to 102
    see also **to**-infinitive
today with the Present Perfect
    and Simple Past 20
to-infinitive
    after a noun 54
    after a verb 54

uncountable nouns 58–60
us 80

verb structures
    verb + **-ing** form 56
    verb + preposition 102
    verb + **to**-infinitive 54
verbs
    irregular verbs 125–26
    passive 50
    sentence structure 4
    suffixes 116
very 94
very much 94
voicing 123

was 12
was allowed to 44
was doing 14
was done *see* passive
we 80
weak forms 124
were 12
were doing 14
will
    in conditionals 106
    future 28, 30
will be allowed to 44
will be done 50
won't
    future 30
word classes 2
word formation 116–17
word order
    adjectives 86, 88
    adverbs 94
    questions 36
    sentence structure 4
worse, worst 91
would
    in conditionals 108, 110

yes
    after a question tag 40
    short answers 38
yes/no questions 36
yet
    with the Present Perfect 18
you 80
    people in general 80
your, yours 74

Zero Conditional 106